Regal Brides

The Astrology of
Five American Women
and their Royal Marriages

Karen Christino

Stella Mira Books
Brooklyn, New York

Acknowledgments

Parts of some chapters of this book were originally published in *Dell Horoscope* and *The Mountain Astrologer* magazines. Many thanks to Ronnie Grishman, Tem Tarriktar, Nan Geary and the staff of both magazines for helping me bring this topic to light.

I've used the astrology program *Solar Fire Gold,* Version 8 for the horoscope charts in this book; thanks to their designers for a versatile program. At times I've used records on *Astrodatabank.com* and I appreciate its presence online. Horoscopes are Geocentric, in the Tropical zodiac, with Placidus houses and the True Nodes. In the absence of a birth time, I generally use noon charts.

The lovely book cover design is by San Coils and *CoverKicks.com.*

Published by Stella Mira Books,
Brooklyn, New York, U.S.A.
StellaMiraBooks@cs.com

ISBN 13: 978-0-9725117-2-8
ISBN 10: 0-9725117-2-5

Table of Contents

Introduction

Royalty doesn't exist the U.S. Though the public and press may treat certain celebrities, wealthy individuals and government officials like royalty, their "reign" lasts only as long as their popularity, money or position holds out. Some do inherit status or cachet from their parents (Paris Hilton and Caroline Kennedy come to mind) but nevertheless don't have any regal responsibilities dictated by birth. Still, many Americans continue to be fascinated by royalty.

A handful of American women have crossed over the line, so to speak. Americans Consuelo Vanderbilt (The Duchess of Marlborough), Wallis Simpson (the Duchess of Windsor), Grace Kelly (Princess Grace of Monaco), Hope Cooke (the Queen of Sikkim) and Lisa Halaby (Queen Noor of Jordan) became royal themselves through their marriages. What led them to their unusual life choices? Are there astrological factors that made them exceptional? Do the wedding charts or compatibility with their royal husbands give an indication of the happiness and success of the marriages?

I became interested in wedding horoscopes when I was writing regularly for *Modern Bride* magazine. The first marriage chart I considered was of course my own. I had the foresight to carefully note the exact time of our vows, but never thought to study the actual chart! When I did, I was dismayed to find that it had not only Mercury retrograde but also a Void of Course Moon. I consider myself very happily married and since we're still together more than 25 years later, I speculated that the wedding chart may be secondary to the birth charts of the bride and groom.

After analyzing hundreds of wedding horoscopes, I'm convinced this is the case. The wedding chart will describe the official union, but it can never override the natal charts or a couple's compatibility. And just as the greatest electional chart for a job interview won't win the position if you don't have the proper experience and credentials, no wedding chart can create a successful marriage if a person has chosen an incompatible partner, isn't ready for a relationship, or isn't able to work on it.

Britney Spears married a childhood friend in Las Vegas with Mercury retrograde and it was annulled two days later: an extreme example of a Mercury retrograde mistake. But Britney also has Aries on the seventh house cusp and Mars in the twelfth house square Neptune, so her overall approach to partnerships may be confused and rash. Paul Newman and Joanne Woodward's marriage had Mars conjunct Saturn as well as the Sun and Venus in a T-square with Uranus and Neptune: a challenging combination that no astrologer would choose. Yet the marriage lasted for over fifty years. David and Victoria Beckham's 1999 marriage features a grand cross of Mercury, Mars, Jupiter and Neptune—along with Saturn in the seventh house square Uranus. If wedding charts were supreme, this relationship would have faltered early on.

I could provide dozens of examples, but suffice it to say that I don't believe that a great wedding date is the glue that keeps a couple together. Nor is a challenging one necessarily the disaster we might fear.

There is also the strange phenomenon of brides gravitating toward the date that they're astrologically "meant to have." I chose wedding dates for clients for a number of years and saw this on a regular basis, and I've heard other astrologers report the same thing. I would ask for unavailable dates up front, and tried for the best days and times. I always provided at least three dates to choose from, but circumstances would often change and they wanted me to come up with something new. I even had some clients manipulate me into approving their own previously selected dates, after paying for better astrological ones! It seemed to me that destiny had a hand in these situations, and it became obvious that the "free will" and supposed choice of an electional chart weren't all that potent.

Still and all, wedding horoscopes, like any birth charts, can be very illustrative. They provide additional information about the bride, the groom and the marriage itself. I was most attracted to studying marriages that were unusual. The weddings of Americans to foreign royalty are especially interesting. They show the significance of the birth charts and compatibility, and this symbolism is often reflected in the wedding charts as well.

Both Jupiter and Saturn are important in the horoscopes of women who marry foreign royals. Jupiter represents the attraction to another culture and people, as well as the possibility of adventures on foreign soil. Saturn relates to status, responsibility, obligations and limitations, which may be more significant for these couples than Jupiter. Saturn can sometimes represent an older, titled or even controlling man, and that symbolism appears as well. The women of these marriages usually have children, which are both a Jupiterian blessing as well as a Saturnine responsibility. And they are generally required to relinquish their U.S. citizenship, which necessitates both embracing new foreign homes (Jupiter) as well as denying the old ones (Saturn).

Notes and Sources:

Britney Spears married Jason Allen Alexander on January 3, 2004 at around 5:00 a.m. in Las Vegas, Nevada. The marriage was annulled 55 hours later according to *People.com*.

Paul Newman and Joanne Woodward were married on January 29, 1958 at 6:00 p.m. in Las Vegas; *Astrodatabank.com* gives no source for the data.

Victoria and David Beckham said "I do" on July 4, 1999 at 4:02 p.m. outside of Dublin, Ireland, as reported by *Geocities.com*.

Consuelo Vanderbilt and the Duke of Marlborough

Consuelo Vanderbilt was one of the most well-known young women of her time. Born on March 2, 1877 to William K. and Alva Vanderbilt, her parents inherited tens of millions when she was just nine years old, and she grew up an heiress.

We don't have a time of birth for Consuelo, so I've set her chart for noon, and it suits her well. With the Sun conjunct Saturn in Pisces, she lived a strict and sheltered life as a girl. Unlike her brothers, she was home-schooled by tutors. Consuelo was literally strapped to a steel rod so she would learn to sit up straight, a vivid image of taskmaster Saturn in her chart, along with Mars conjunct Jupiter in the sign of Capricorn. Her mother, Alva, was a formidable Victorian woman with the Sun closely conjunct Mars in Capricorn, and both squaring her Pluto in Aries. She insisted on obedience and used a riding whip as punishment for minor infringements of the rules. Consuelo and her mother shared Mars in Capricorn, but Alva was the disciplinarian and Consuelo the disciplined child.

Consuelo's Sun conjunct Saturn in Pisces made her kind and earnest. Many commented on her simplicity and quiet dignity. She had formal manners, but was sweet and compassionate. Even as an elderly woman, she had an elegant and dignified presence in photos, and friends and acquaintances said she always retained a youthfulness of spirit.

Consuelo Vanderbilt
March 2, 1877, New York, New York; noon chart
Source: *Consuelo and Alva Vanderbilt.*

Consuelo was a solitary girl who was easily upset by her parents' disagreements, which began early in her life. Pisces is sensitive and Saturn takes things very seriously. The Sun conjunct Saturn can also impose limitations and indicate issues with parental authority figures, particularly the father. Consuelo's father reportedly had many love affairs, and William and Alva were divorced when Consuelo was eighteen.

Ambitious Capricorn Alva was determined that her daughter marry a European aristocrat, as a number of other American heiresses had already done. She thought that a royal marriage would give Consuelo a permanent career in life and ensure her a responsible role in society. Meanwhile, the girl had met and fallen in love with a common American. On her eighteenth birthday, he secretly proposed and she accepted. Her independent Venus in Aquarius opposite Uranus seemed to be asserting itself. She would have fallen in love quickly and with someone who shared her interests and ideas.

Alva soon took Consuelo to Europe to meet some eligible men. Tall, graceful and slim with dark hair and a sweet face, Consuelo epitomized the "Gibson Girl" look. Along with friends, mother and daughter were invited by Charles Spencer-Churchill, the Duke of Marlborough, to visit him at his English country estate. With Consuelo's Capricorn planets and Sun conjunct Saturn, she was a dutiful daughter who followed her mother's instructions.

When mother and daughter returned to their summer home in Newport, Rhode Island, Alva invited the Duke to visit, and he proposed on August 23, 1895. Consuelo quickly told her mother of her previous commitment and Alva just as quickly kept Consuelo from all contact with anyone outside the household. When Consuelo continued to object to the arranged marriage, her mother threatened to shoot her American fiancé. Alva then had a friend tell Consuelo that her mother had suffered a heart attack as a result of the argument. What would any Pisces teenager do when faced with such a domineering Capricorn parent? She went along with the plan.

The wedding was scheduled to be held in six weeks and Consuelo was kept in virtual confinement, once again symbolized by her Pisces Sun and Saturn. Her English governess convinced the idealistic Pisces girl that her new position would allow her a role of great social service. This idea must have appealed to her humanitarian-minded Mercury and Venus in Aquarius.

Why was the Duke of Marlborough so intent on Consuelo as a bride? He desperately needed money. His father had run down Blenheim, their family estate, having sold the library, many valuable paintings, and porcelain. His parents divorced and the father subsequently married a wealthy American widow to support his spending habits. (Charles' uncle also married an American, Jennie Jerome; their son, Winston Churchill, was his first cousin.)

With the Sun in Scorpio opposing Pluto in Taurus, the Duke was a realist who must have been keenly aware of the need to revive his name and replenish his property. His Mars conjunct Saturn in Capricorn made him perhaps even more of a hard-nosed businessperson than Alva was.

The Duke's Mercury in Scorpio was insightful, and with a trine to Jupiter in Cancer, he knew exactly where to get the funds. He made a deal with William K. Vanderbilt for a $2.5 million dowry (still a tremendous sum today, over a hundred years later). The money would go toward renovating the estate. But the Duke was also promised $100,000 a year for life from Consuelo's father, a figure equivalent to over $2 million a year today. And this settlement had no strings attached. No matter what happened with Consuelo, it was guaranteed income. The wedding went ahead as planned.

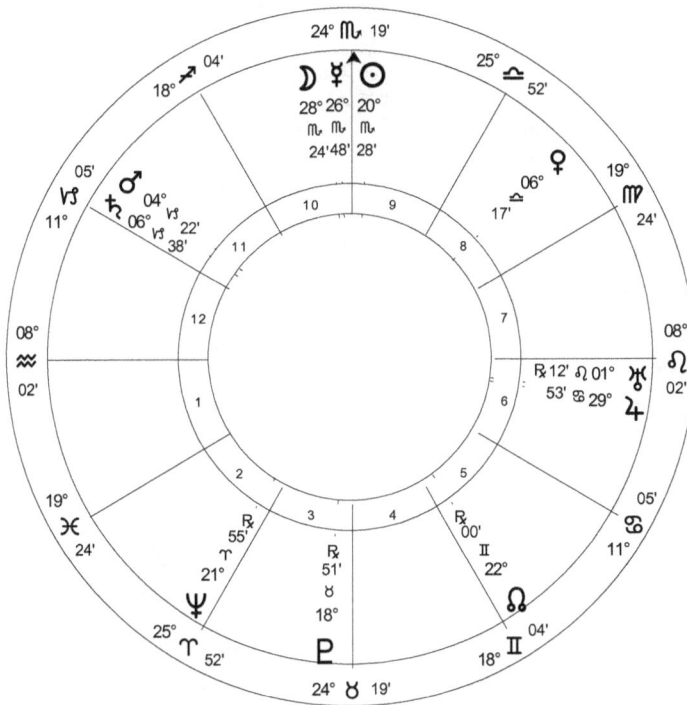

Charles Spencer-Churchill
November 13, 1871, Simla, India; noon chart
Source: *Wikipedia.com.*

The emotional intensity of this event can be seen in the wedding chart. The Sun, Mars and Saturn were all in Scorpio and squaring Jupiter. The Sun conjunct Saturn in Scorpio in the wedding chart looks more like a commercial transaction than a marriage. This coupling reflects both of their charts: Consuelo's Sun conjunct Saturn and the Duke's Sun in Scorpio. Jupiter in Leo is conjunct the descendent and epitomizes the enormous publicity the event received. The streets were crowded with fans and police, and the wedding had been the hottest gossip to hit newspapers and magazines in the weeks since the announcement.

Consuelo Marries the Duke of Marlborough
November 6, 1895, approximately 12:45 p.m., New York, NY.
Source: *The New York Times* stated that the wedding began at
noon; a large bridal party entered and a service was held
before the ceremony.

Consuelo spent the morning alone in tears and a
reporter from the *New York Herald* observed beneath her
veil that she had been crying. The Sun conjunct Uranus
in the wedding chart shows an unusual, and perhaps
unsteady, union. Though their ages were similar (his 25
years to her 18) observers noted that Consuelo was half
a head taller than her new husband (he was just 5'2", she
5'8"). She was beautiful and he appeared pale and frail.

Consuelo was now a Duchess; she moved to England
with her husband and became a member of a very

hierarchical society. With her strong Saturn and Capricorn planets, she was already accustomed to discipline and structure. But she also found the Duke less than congenial. His Mars conjunct Saturn in Capricorn made him acutely aware of status and reputation; he was quite class-conscious and felt innately superior to others. He probably also felt a sense of power from his position, as his Sun in Scorpio trine Jupiter had naturally given him. Consuelo, with her Pisces Sun conjunct Saturn and Aquarius planets, was modest, with a love for all humanity. Her own experience had given her a desire to help those who were suffering or less fortunate. It soon also became apparent that the Duke looked down on Americans as well. Some rather negative Scorpio characteristics are often used to describe him, such as suspicious and vindictive. He had a domineering streak and was self-absorbed.

The Duke's Mars conjunct Saturn squared his Venus in Libra: he had good taste and considered himself a connoisseur, but criticized his accomplished wife and rarely complimented her. He must have appreciated Consuelo's beauty and charm, but had sacrificed a more rewarding union to practicality. He also did not appear to have the intellectual capabilities or interests that Consuelo had.

A wedding chart not only describes the wedding day itself, but also symbolizes the marriage to come. The Sun indicates the groom and the Moon the bride. In the Vanderbilt-Marlborough wedding horoscope, the Sun conjoined with Saturn and Uranus in Scorpio symbolizes the Duke and his autocratic and controlling behavior, as well as their unusual joining of interests. On their honeymoon, Consuelo was exposed to prostitutes who seemed to know her husband, as well as social jealousy and ostentatious spending: some very Scorpionic issues. Scorpio is complex emotionally and they both admitted in an early quarrel that they had been in love with another.

The Moon placed in its ruling sign of Cancer in the wedding chart shows that Consuelo provided the heart and soul of this union. Since the Moon falls in the fifth house of children, she had two sons within about three years of her marriage (the "heir and a spare,"a phrase she may have coined). The Moon's trines to Saturn and Mars show that Consuelo would take her responsibilities seriously, and she did. Her London debut in 1896 was a great success. She became responsible for a 170-room palace and forty servants.

In a wedding horoscope, the Ascendant indicates the person who proposes. Here, the Aquarius Ascendant is traditionally ruled by Saturn and represents the Duke. In contemporary interpretation, Uranus would rule Aquarius, and both Saturn and Uranus are conjunct the Sun—all signifying the Duke. The seventh house then represents Consuelo, where we have Jupiter in Leo symbolizing the famous heiress. Jupiter squares both the Sun and Saturn and is also in square to Uranus by sign, all showing the couple's challenging compatibility. Consuelo found the protocol and ritual of English aristocracy stifling (Jupiter square Saturn). Ultimately, the couple had very little in common, with completely different points of view and incompatible temperaments.

In romantic relationships, Mars aspecting Mars is often considered positive synastry. But while the Marlboroughs shared Mars conjunct each other's Mars in early Capricorn, the Duke's Saturn also conjoined

Consuelo's Mars and Jupiter. This probably cooled her feelings. He had given her a position in English society, but also limited her freedom. Venus combinations often promise compatibility, but Charles' Venus in Libra squared his wife's Mars, and her Venus and Mercury in Aquarius squared his Pluto, showing their very different tastes and temperaments.

Consuelo believed that the wealthy were duty-bound to alleviate the suffering of others, and she began doing charitable work, first for the tenants on the estate and little by little in larger venues. This was wonderful for her Pisces-Aquarius nature. She organized a project to help prisoners' wives gain independence and eventually campaigned for women's rights, among many other projects.

In 1901, the Duke fell in love with Consuelo's good friend Gladys Deacon, and probably had an affair. At around the same time, Consuelo may have had an affair with a French painter. The couple were legally separated in 1906; the marriage had lasted nearly eleven years. (If we look at the wedding horoscope like a horary chart, there are about eleven degrees between Jupiter and Uranus, figuratively showing when Consuelo was released to freedom.) There were no allegations of infidelity, and Consuelo was granted custody of her children for six months a year, unusual for the time. The Duke and Duchess lived separate lives until the boys were grown, when Consuelo filed a petition for divorce.

The wedding Sun conjunct Saturn and Mars in Scorpio, all squaring the Ascendant, presented a challenging marriage, but one that was also difficult to undo. Scorpio is tenacious and the wedding Ascendant was also in Aquarius, another fixed sign. Consuelo and the Duke were required to go through an elaborate legal process to finally divorce in 1921. Shortly after that the Duke married Gladys.

Meanwhile, Consuelo had met French aviator Jacques Balsan, a much better match. They were married on July 4, 1921, and shared a happy life together in the French countryside. Yet Jacques' family was Catholic, and would not accept a divorced woman. Consuelo decided to have her first marriage annulled by the Catholic Church. In her official statement, she said that her mother had coerced her to marry the Duke and that she was underage at the time. The church granted the annulment and Consuelo and Jacques were married for a second time in a Catholic ceremony on November 25, 1926. The complicated Scorpio marriage had actually taken twenty years and three separate legal actions to completely dissolve: the 1906 separation, 1921 divorce and 1926 annulment.

Since we have no birth time for Consuelo, it's difficult to consider the specifics of her marriages astrologically. But the Sun and Saturn reflect the men in our lives. With the Sun conjunct Saturn, Consuelo gained status through her first marriage, but also had much responsibility and little satisfaction with the Duke. Her second marriage was more rewarding, but she had to wait until the age of 44 to formalize it. Saturn may take time to manifest, but it can pay off if we have patience.

The Duke died in 1934. Consuelo and Jacques supported local children and hospitals in the early years of World War II, but returned to the United States in 1940. They lived happily together until his death in 1956. Consuelo died in 1964 at the age of 87 and was buried in England next to her younger son.

Notes and Sources:

Balsan, Consuelo Vanderbilt, *The Glitter & the Gold*. George Mann Books, Kent, England, 1953.

Stuart, Amanda, *Consuelo and Alva Vanderbilt*. Harper-Collins, New York, 2006.

Alva Vanderbilt was born on January 17, 1853 in Mobile, Alabama according to *Consuelo and Alva Vanderbilt*.

Wallis Simpson and the Duke of Windsor

In 1936, Wallis Warfield Simpson was named *Time* magazine's "Woman of the Year," the first time for a woman since the feature premiered. An American socialite, Simpson had become widely known as the companion of England's King Edward VIII. But as a divorcée, she was not eligible to marry him. In early December, 1936, Wallis publicly claimed that she would give up the King rather than jeopardize his position. But he nevertheless announced his decision to abdicate the throne for the woman he loved. Many viewed the situation as a modern love story. Dozens of books have been written about the couple, and their romance has inspired several television movies. It is certainly a dramatic tale.

How did a poor American rise to become the wife of an English royal? What was their marriage really like? Mystery and speculation surround the couple, but astrology can help us analyze both of the personalities as well as their marriage to learn more about them.

Wallis Simpson was born on June 19, 1896 in Blue Ridge Summit, Pennsylvania. Her early life was often difficult. Her parents married when she was several months old and her father died from tuberculosis a year later. She and her mother lived with and were supported by her grandmother, uncle and aunt. When Wallis was twelve, her mother remarried an alcoholic; he died within five years. But Wallis transformed herself from a tomboy into a confident, bold teenager. She was a good dancer and though she lacked classically good looks, many young men found her attractive.

The Sun symbolizes men and the triple conjunction of the Sun, Venus and Neptune all in Gemini suggests the loss of her father, as well as her step-father's alcoholism. Although the Sun-Neptune conjunction is a little wide, Neptune may show confusing circumstances and nebulous relationships. It's also typically associated with drinking or substance abuse. Wallis' own taste, talent and personal charisma, however, are evident in this important planetary combination, which gave her a strong sense of romance.

Wallis Simpson
June 19, 1896, 7:00 a.m., Blue Ridge Summit, Pennsylvania.
Source: Rectified by Blanca Holmes, *Wynn's Astrology Magazine*, October 1944 from 6:00 to 7:00 a.m. given by Wallis

Her Moon in Libra in her fourth house shows the importance of her early life and family. She had some lucky breaks due to the Moon's sextile to Jupiter, and her uncle paid for her to attend an exclusive girls' school in Baltimore (since Jupiter is the general significator of education). The Moon's trines to eleventh house Mercury, Neptune and Pluto increased her allure, making her sociable and friendly, and the Moon's opposition to Mars in Aries gave her the drive to excel. She was known for her charm and ability to talk to anyone (Libra and Gemini qualities), as well as her exquisite taste (Jupiter in Leo in the first house).

Wallis married Win Spencer, a U.S. Navy officer, on November 8, 1916. They were married for over ten years, but the relationship was marred by his alcoholism and their frequent separations. We can see Wallis' Sun-Venus-Neptune pattern repeating itself in this relationship. More specifically, Saturn rules her seventh house of partnerships, and becomes the significator of her first marriage. It strongly squared Jupiter, Wallis' own significator in her first house, so she could be at odds with her husband, especially early in life (she was just 20 at the time). But Jupiter's influence is clear, since Wallis traveled to many ports with Win, including San Diego, Washington and Hong Kong. The couple divorced in 1927. Wallis was rumored to have had many affairs, which would not be surprising with her Sun, Venus and Neptune conjunct in mutable Gemini. Uranus in Scorpio was also in her fifth house at the apex of a yod involving Venus (love) and Mars (the natural indicator of sexuality and the ruler of her Scorpio fifth house). Mercury retrograde closely conjunct Neptune may have given her romantic ideals, but also the possibility of faulty judgment, especially when young.

Much of Wallis' life was spent in transit, and it's easy to see why. With so much Gemini, she must have had a restless spirit and a curiosity about the world. Her Jupiter in Leo sextile her Moon suggests a need to explore, as well as a personal thirst for adventure. The Moon opposed to Mars also points toward habits of movement and action.

Wallis soon married her second husband, Ernest Simpson, a shipping executive, on July 21, 1928 in London. He was a much more stable man, and though many of their U.S. investments were lost in the 1929 stock market crash, Simpson's business interests in Europe and Scandinavia kept the couple secure.

With Mars in Aries in the tenth house of reputation, and Mercury and Neptune in the eleventh of society, Wallis Simpson had always been socially ambitious. Mercury also conjoined Pluto in the eleventh house in her birth chart, and her many connections may have been something of an obsession. They also transformed her life. Her friend, Lady Furness (formerly the American Thelma Morgan), was the Prince of Wales' mistress, and she introduced Wallis to him in 1931. The Prince was the oldest son of George V and Queen Mary, and next in line for the English throne. With his royal status and eligibility, he had been in the news continuously for several years.

The Prince's Sun was in Cancer and trined the Moon in Pisces. The Moon in his first house made him sympathetic, and highlighted the role of family in his life. He loved children and the poor and was considered to be more natural and informal than other royals of his day. His Mars in Aries, closely trining his Sagittarius Midheaven, shows his military success on the French front during World War I.

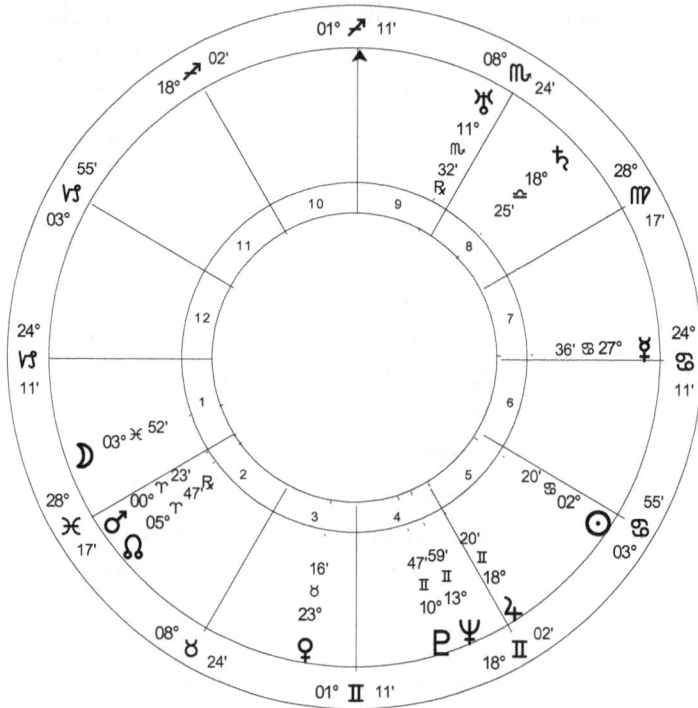

The Duke of Windsor
June 23, 1894 at 9:55 p.m., Richmond, England.
Source: Birth record and official time.

But sympathetic Mercury in Cancer on his seventh house cusp formed a grand trine with both Mars and the Midheaven and left him with a revulsion to the destructive powers of war. In the 1930s, many Europeans feared the Communists in Russia. Some, like the Prince of Wales, preferred the Nazis and Fascists to the Communist threat. In a 1935 speech to WWI veterans, the Prince famously recommended that the conflicts of the past should be forgotten and suggested that Nazi Germany posed no threat.

While Wallis was still married to Ernest Simpson, the couple socialized with the Prince's set, and she began her love affair with him. Her impressionable Neptune, conjoining both Mercury and Venus, must have been smitten with being swept away in a romantic fairy tale. The Prince, with Venus in Taurus trine his Capricorn Ascendant, was a more realistic partner. But Neptune and Jupiter straddling his fifth house cusp also made him a romantic, and his rising Moon in Pisces accentuated these feelings. He could have been sentimental or even misguided about love. It seems as if both parties simply ignored the reality of their situations; she was already married, and if he wanted to inherit the throne, he would need a suitable wife.

Wallis and the Prince did have many wonderful astrological combinations. Though she was Gemini and he Cancer, their birthdays were only four days apart, so their Suns were conjunct. Her Sun also trined his Moon, an aspect traditionally associated with compatibility. Connections between Venus and Mars offer sexual chemistry, and if not aspected with each other in their charts, her Venus conjunct his Sun created a likeable companionship. His Venus in Taurus opposite her Uranus in Scorpio made her exciting and alluring to him. Her Mars square his Mercury and his Mars square her Sun created a strong dynamic that probably went beyond sexual attraction. Some astrologers might consider these aspects harsh or grating, but for two individuals with competitive and headstrong Mars in Aries in their birth charts, these squares indicate a certain amount of excitement. Both could regard the other as a personality to be reckoned with.

All of these inter-aspects gave Wallis and the Prince attraction and compatibility, but it is Saturn that usually makes a relationship last. The Prince's Saturn trined Wallis' Sun and Venus and conjoined her Moon. Her Saturn trined both his Sun and Moon. While several of these aspects are somewhat wide (up to ten degrees from exact), they still add stability, security and shared responsibility to the relationship. And since both parties' Saturns are involved, they would each feel committed to the union. Aspects like these, particularly the Prince's Saturn conjunct Wallis' Moon, were especially necessary for the relationship to last, since Wallis' many planets in mutable Gemini made her changeable.

The Prince's seventh house Mercury also conjoins her Ascendant. This shows that she represented exactly what he was looking for in a mate.

On January 19, 1936, King George V died, making the Prince the new King, Edward VIII. While royals throughout history have had love affairs, Edward accompanied Wallis in public, flouting convention. His Sun and Moon in water signs show that his emotional life was most important. His first house Moon trine Uranus in the ninth also made him representative of a more modern generation, especially since Uranus is the most elevated planet in his horoscope. And Jupiter and Neptune conjunct his fifth house cusp gave him a blind spot where his affections were concerned.

King Edward actually wanted to marry Wallis. The King is the head of the Church of England and the Church did not permit those with former spouses who were still alive to remarry. Wallis' first husband was living, and of course, she was still married to Ernest Simpson! Many also viewed Mrs. Simpson as a woman of limitless ambition. With Mars in the aggressive sign of Aries in her tenth house sextile Neptune, along with Jupiter in Leo in her first house trine the Midheaven, this seems like an apt assessment.

The government and Prime Minister would not allow the King to be crowned until the issue was settled. Wallis began divorce proceedings. Then, on December 7, 1936, Edward VIII announced his decision to abdicate. He agreed to leave the country and had to receive special permission from the government in order to return. Edward now became the Duke of Windsor; he had been King for less than a year.

The Duke's horoscope does not seem like a particularly challenging one. His Midheaven, showing status and reputation, formed a grand trine with Mars in his second house and Mercury. Mercury was placed in Cancer and conjoined his seventh house, representing the public, who had great affection for him. But Jupiter in the fifth house rules his Sagittarius Midheaven, so his affections (the fifth house) had determined the direction of his life and career (as ruler of the tenth). And Jupiter is of course conjunct nebulous, vague and at times misguided Neptune.

Wallis received her divorce in October of 1936, but it would not be finalized for another six months. During that difficult time, she consulted an astrologer in Switzerland (who might have been Karl Ernst Krafft, a Nazi sympathizer who would later work for Joseph Goebbels). She was given a written horoscope that depressed her, as it forecast many obstacles ahead. At the time, Saturn in Pisces was transiting her ninth house of legal, religious and international affairs, and would square all of her Gemini planets over the next six months. However, on May 3, 1937, the divorce was final. The Duke's younger brother was crowned George VI on May 12; the Duke and Wallis were not invited.

The couple planned a June wedding near Paris, their new home, and received wedding gifts from Hitler and Mussolini. The Duke was deeply hurt that no member of the royal family was permitted to attend. Wallis' only family member present was her Aunt Bessie.

They had beautiful weather at a French chateau for the small wedding and light buffet lunch. The time of a marriage's start is a key astrological question. Most, myself included, believe it begins with the words "I do" that seal the agreement. But in France, both a civil and a religious ceremony are often required. Which chart do we use? This may depend upon how religious the parties are, or what they consider most meaningful. In this case, however, the religious ceremony began right after the civil ceremony, so the horoscopes do not differ very much.

The wedding chart describes the situation well (see next page). The first house, usually representing the man, has Neptune squaring the Sun in the tenth. What could be a more appropriate pattern for a man who had sacrificed his position for love? In his natal chart, the Duke had the Moon in Pisces in the first house square his Midheaven, lending a similar flavor. Other combinations in the wedding chart also show similarities with the birth charts of the couple and their inter-aspects. The Duke had Saturn in his eighth house trining Jupiter in the fifth at birth. In the wedding chart, Saturn is once again placed in the eighth, this time sextiling Jupiter in the fifth, connecting the two planets, as they are in his horoscope. Wallis' natal Moon conjoined Saturn in the Duke's eighth house, and the wedding Moon is also conjunct Saturn in the wedding chart (in Pisces, the same sign as the Duke's own Moon).

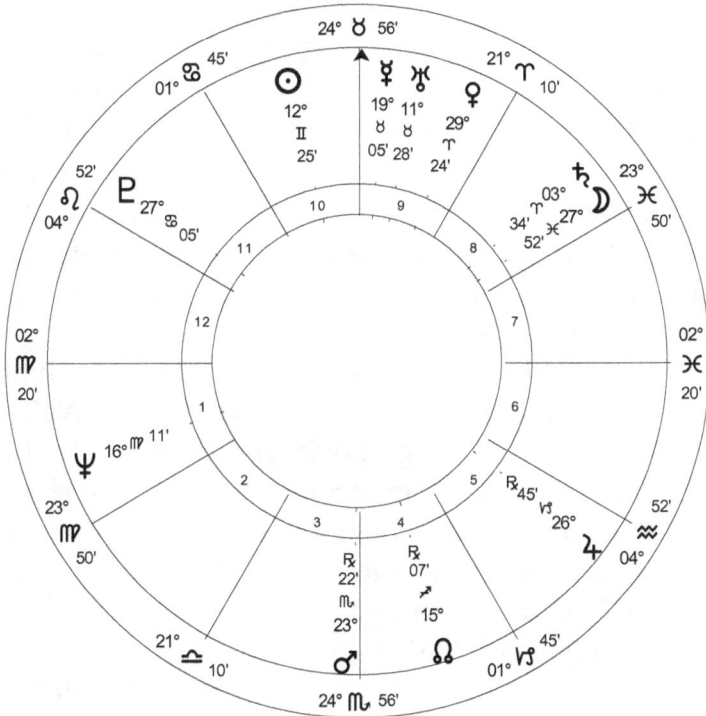

Wallis Marries the Duke of Windsor
June 3, 1937, 11:42 a.m., Monts, France;
the religious ceremony began at noon.
Source: *The Duchess of Windsor: the Secret Life*.

The wedding chart features a kite pattern based on a grand trine between the Moon conjunct Saturn, Mars in Scorpio and Pluto in Cancer. Jupiter then forms the top of the kite by opposing Pluto and sextiling Mars, the Moon and Saturn. The kite is usually considered a favorable pattern, but the malefics Mars, Saturn and Pluto are all involved, and Jupiter in its detriment in Capricorn is not at its best (consider its influence in 2008 with a tumbling real estate market and financial crisis in the U.S.).

Since the Moon often represents the woman in a wedding chart, Wallis is in an unfortunate position. The Moon is not strong in the sign of Pisces and is limited by its conjunction with Saturn and placement in the eighth house. Wallis had become a Duchess, but she was now completely dependent upon the Duke. Before the wedding, she signed a marriage contract that stipulated their property was to be kept entirely separate. With Saturn in his eighth in his own birth chart, as well as Saturn's flowing aspects in the wedding horoscope, the Duke no doubt felt obligated to fulfill his responsibilities to those closest to him. But it must have stung Wallis to have achieved such a high position in society only to be robbed of any right to joint property with her husband.

Many writers have made much of the Duke and Duchess' pro-Nazi sympathies. The Duke met with Hitler in 1937 and also had dinner with Rudolf Hess. European alliances that were solidified in later years were already lining up. Although many at the time did not foresee Germany's tremendous ambition, some speculated that if the current government of Great Britain rejected Hitler, the Duke could be returned to the throne under German influence or control. In a wedding chart, the couple's philosophy, ideals and political beliefs are represented by the ninth house. In Wallis' marriage to the Duke, these are represented by Mercury in Taurus in the ninth opposed to Mars in Scorpio on the fourth house cusp. Their beliefs (ninth house) threatened their stability (fourth house) and were complicated by family relationships (also a fourth house matter). Since Mercury trines the rising Neptune, they may have been deceived or misguided.

The couple had no children. Jupiter's placement in the wedding's fifth house in Capricorn and also ruling the seventh suggests the bride's mature age. Wallis was 41 at the time of the marriage, and she has been accused of having an early abortion that destroyed her fertility. Whatever their actual history, independent Uranus in her fifth house of children is at the apex of the yod with Venus and Mars, and she never related well to children. The wedding chart has Jupiter in the fifth house, and while it's at the point of the wedding chart's kite, it's also part of a T-square created by an opposition with Pluto and squares to Venus. This is a stressful pattern that includes Jupiter in its detriment in Capricorn and Venus in its detriment in Aries. The sign of Capricorn is on the fifth house cusp and Saturn rules it. The Moon conjunct Saturn in the eighth house also presents similar limitations. My guess is that Wallis might have conceived but could not maintain a pregnancy. The Duke, a family-oriented Cancer who also had the Moon rising in his birth chart, had given up much more than the throne.

With England's entry into World War II in 1939, the Duke of Windsor was appointed to assess the French defense, but felt it was a nominal position; he wanted to be doing something more significant. In July of 1940, he was offered the governorship of the Bahamas, probably a tactic to send him away from the focus of the action and keep his pro-German views in check. While there, he was outspoken against British government policies. He also remained bitter about his family's treatment of him. Mars in Scorpio conjunct the fourth house in the wedding chart opposes Mercury and shows the complexities of his family, and is a good example of the intensity and durability of fixed sign dynamics. As the war wound down in 1945, the Duke resigned his post and the couple returned to France.

In the late 1940s Wallis and the Duke lived in Paris and traveled between the south of France, London and New York. Wallis was said to have frequent periods of depression; her own chart had first house Jupiter square Saturn. Her feelings may not have been simply the result of her own internal conflicts between freedom and authority. Depression is also indicated by the Duke's Saturn conjoining her Moon and the wedding chart's Moon conjunct Saturn. Her condition could have been exacerbated by her marriage and relationship with her husband.

The Duke was eventually able to draw closer to his family. King George VI died in 1952 and young Queen Elizabeth seemed to want to make peace with her uncle. He died in 1972 and was buried near Windsor Castle. Wallis lived until she was nearly 90 years old. By then she had lost much of her memory, but was buried next to her husband in 1986. In death, she had finally achieved her ambition to become an integral part of the royal family.

Notes and Sources:

Higham, Charles, *The Duchess of Windsor: The Secret Life*. McGraw Hill, New York, 1988.

King, Greg, *The Duchess of Windsor*. Citadel Press, New York, 1999.

Grace Kelly and the Prince of Monaco

Grace Kelly was Hollywood's golden girl in the 1950s. Elegant, poised and aristocratic, Kelly was a screen phenomenon from her first starring role, and appeared in a string of hits opposite top leading men for five years, winning a Best Actress Oscar in 1955. To cap off her incredible career, she married Monaco's Prince Rainier in 1956 and became Princess Grace. While many Scorpio women have the tenacity and drive to rise to top acting roles (Jodie Foster, Julia Roberts, Demi Moore, Calista Flockhart and Anne Hathaway, to name a few), none today can touch the success of Grace Kelly. She epitomized the ideal of her time, which included marriage and children.

Grace was born on November 12, 1929 and came from a wealthy background, as her father was the head of the largest brick masonry firm in the U.S. He was also a sports enthusiast and three-time Olympic gold medal winner, and her mother was an athletics teacher. Grace, her two brothers and sister were encouraged to excel, and she had regular ballet and swimming lessons as a girl. But she was more interested in acting, and when she graduated from high school, she moved to New York City and enrolled at the American Academy of Dramatic Arts.

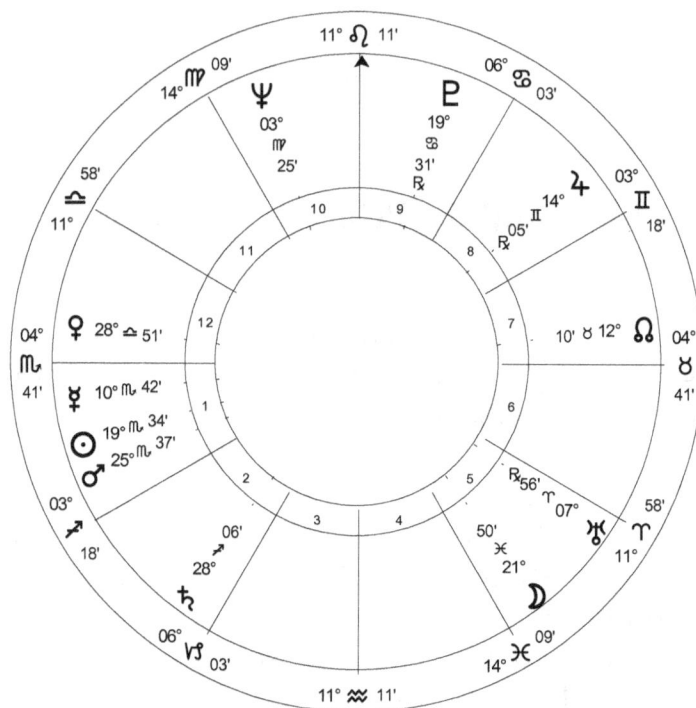

Grace Kelly
November 12, 1929 at 5:31 a.m., Philadelphia, Pennsylvania.
Source: Birth Certificate and *Astrodatabank*.

By the time she was 19, Grace was posing as a model for magazines and TV commercials. She worked in summer stock and was in a Broadway show at 20. Her arresting personality and appearance are evident in her horoscope. With the Sun, Mercury and Mars in the first house in Scorpio, she had a charismatic and magnetic presence. Though she also had Scorpio rising, Venus in Libra conjoined the Ascendant, giving her even features and a polished personality. She was elegant and poised, with a sophisticated air. The Sun conjunct Mars in Scorpio also provided the drive to make something of herself; these planets formed a grand trine with the Moon in Pisces in the fifth house of creativity and Pluto in the ninth of wide appeal. Grace had what many astrologers would call an "easy" chart for success. While a grand water trine has the potential to be lazy or overly sensitive, her first house Mars gave her ambition and focus. Venus rising and the Ascendant, both sextiling Neptune in the tenth, allowed her to express her feelings through an artistic career. Mercury in the first house squaring the Midheaven in Leo made her a communicator with a dramatic flair that people noticed. Since Leo and Scorpio are fixed signs, she was quite committed to her goals. Mercury also rules her eleventh house of hopes and wishes for the future.

By 1950 Grace had landed her first film, and the following year she appeared in her breakout role in *High Noon*, starring opposite Gary Cooper, nearly thirty years her senior. MGM immediately signed her to a seven-year contract; she was just 22. Transiting Uranus in Cancer had begun activating her grand trine from the ninth house, galvanizing the public's attention toward her and bringing many exciting adventures her way.

Over the next several years, Grace Kelly reinforced her position as a leading lady. She starred with Clark Gable in *Mogambo*. Alfred Hitchcock directed her opposite Ray Milland in *Dial M for Murder*, with James Stewart in *Rear Window*, and in *To Catch a Thief* with Cary Grant. She played opposite William Holden and Bing Crosby in *A Country Girl* in 1954. All of these are remembered as classic films, and Kelly became a female icon. Yet her co-stars had all been much older men. Perhaps this is because Saturn, representing the establishment, closely sextiled Kelly's rising Venus and trined her tenth house Neptune. It also squared her creative fifth house Moon, one of the few challenging aspects in her horoscope.

There were many rumors that Grace had love affairs with her leading men. Gossipy magazines and books tend to exaggerate, but Grace's horoscope suggests the rumors could be true. The Moon in Pisces in her fifth house gave her many talents, but also a strong sense of romance. As a mutable sign, Pisces, especially when young, would be comfortable with a variety of partners. Jupiter in the eighth house of sexuality is also in a mutable sign, Gemini, and its sextile to Uranus in Aries may delight in romantic conquest. The strong planets rising in Scorpio also reinforce this interpretation. She was a young woman and must have been thrilled at the idea of a more intimate involvement with some of the most powerful men in Hollywood.

Grace Kelly was at the height of her career on March 30, 1955 and only 25 when she won a Best Actress Oscar for her performance in *A Country Girl*. The planets combined to make for a once-in-a-lifetime event. Transiting Uranus was stationary at 23-½° Cancer, trining both her Moon and Mars and energizing her grand trine from the ninth house. Transiting Jupiter at 20° Cancer conjoined transiting Uranus as it stationed in the sign of its exaltation, also boosting her close grand trine of the Sun, Moon and Pluto. If that were not enough, Saturn in Scorpio had recently turned retrograde at 21°, conjoining her first house Sun and solidifying her career while activating the natal trines as well. Transiting Saturn often repays us for past efforts and Grace was able to capitalize on all of her hard work in the previous seven years. Transiting Neptune conjunct her natal Venus magically rewarded her for her artistic efforts.

Scorpios are often intrigued by metaphysical studies and the occult, and Kelly's biographer Wendy Leigh says that Grace consulted Hollywood astrologer Carroll Righter for more than twenty years. It's fascinating to imagine him analyzing her horoscope, perhaps with the question of whether she would win the Academy Award, as this incredible combination of planetary influences unfolded.

Only a little over a month later, Grace attended the Cannes Film Festival and briefly met Prince Rainier of Monaco. Later that year, she filmed a picture called *The Swan*, in which she played a princess. Transiting Neptune remained close to her natal Venus, making her the perfect person to embody a romantic fantasy. After Kelly's return home, she corresponded with the Prince and saw him again as he visited mutual friends; he had dinner at home with the Kelly family on December 14, 1955. The next day, the couple became engaged, announcing the news a few weeks later. Grace was 26; the Prince, 32. With transiting Jupiter now stationing conjunct her tenth house Neptune, Grace seemed to be living out the romantic fantasy.

Grace's fiancé, Prince Rainier, was born on May 31, 1923. He ruled over Monaco's 370 acres (about half the size of New York City's Central Park), just east of Nice on the French Rivera. Casino gambling had been authorized in Monaco a century before, when it was banned in France and Italy. But by the 1950s the little principality was in decline. Greek shipping magnate Ari Onassis had recently bought up the casino interests in the area. In order to revitalize their businesses, Onassis suggested that the Prince consider marrying a famous actress who'd popularize Monaco. He suggested Eva Marie Saint, Deborah Kerr and even Marilyn Monroe. And then the Prince met Grace Kelly.

The Prince had the Sun, Mercury and possibly the Ascendant in Gemini, which may be the most different sign in the zodiac from Scorpio! He was light and changeable while Grace was deep. But her Jupiter in the eighth house was also in Gemini and conjoined his Sun. Financial interests were a part of their experience together, and her father paid him a $2 million dowry. His Jupiter in Scorpio also conjoined her first house Sun and Mercury, so Jupiter's benefits were mutual.

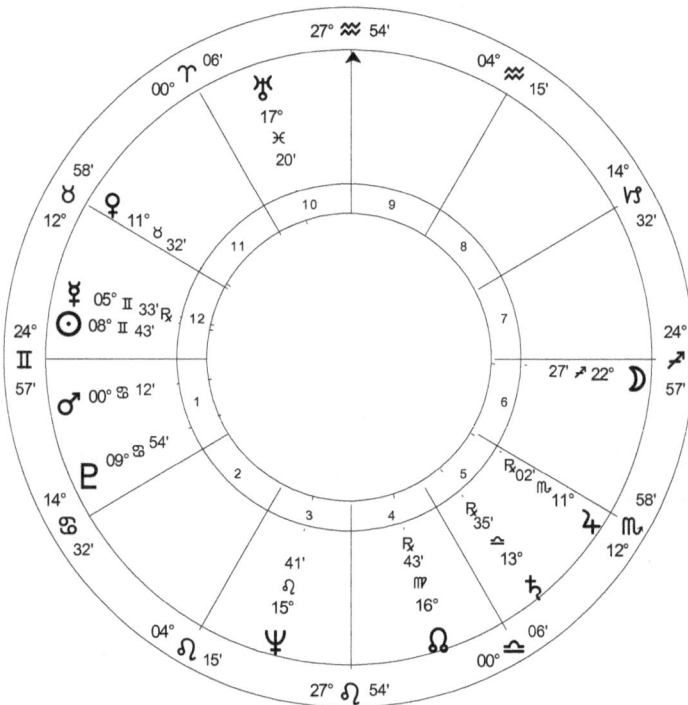

Prince Rainier
May 31, 1923, 6:00 a.m., Monte Carlo, Monaco. Source: *Astrodatabank* cites the Church of Light and *World Astrology*.

The Prince's Moon in Sagittarius closely squared Grace's Pisces Moon, so they had different habits, perspectives and lifestyles. Yet his Moon also conjoined her Saturn, suggesting that she would provide the element of stability in the relationship; financial stability was a part of that since Grace's Saturn was in her second house.

The Prince's Uranus at 17° Pisces trined Grace's Sun and conjoined her fifth house Moon, and he certainly brought an element of excitement and change into her life as Uranus is wont to do. She must have found him exciting and charming when they first met.

Grace had already agreed to star in the movie *High Society* with Frank Sinatra, and filming went ahead in January of 1956. When it was over, she departed by ocean liner from New York harbor on April 4, 1956 for her wedding in Monaco.

Why would Grace Kelly give up an incredibly successful career and stake it all on a relatively minor royal? Maybe transiting Neptune had turned her head and made her actually believe she was in a fairy tale. But natal Neptune in her tenth house probably also gave her a need to find something more than simple financial success. She may have grown tired of all the travel and short-term relationships that were often part of movie-making. Her career had come so easily to her and the romantic illusion may have worn off. She already had money, fame and success. One could argue that at 26, she'd done it all. A Scorpio actress in today's world might turn to producing or directing, like Demi Moore or Jodie Foster. These things were not such viable options for most actresses in the 1950s.

Grace Kelly had an easy, flowing horoscope and may have taken the path of least resistance. But if we look at her chart, we can also see that she's not really a careerist. With all of her first house planets, she was more interested in self-development and reaching her greatest potential. The ruler of her tenth house, the Sun, comes to the first: her career had come to her, and not the other way around. She was a striking personality and would continue to be one, even after retiring from her life as a film star.

Grace's main reason for settling down may have been her desire for a family. In marrying a prince, she would insure a secure position in society for her children. Show business, as she must have known from her own experience, has never been known for its stability. Scorpio values intimate relationships, and the maternal Moon in the fifth house is a classic signature of a caring mother. Grace's Moon in Pisces is tender and supportive, and since it had mostly flowing aspects, being a mother would be something that came naturally to her. In the 1950s, the age of 26 was not considered nearly as young as it is today. Medical advances that allow women like Julia Roberts and Calista Flockhart to postpone children were not yet available.

In a William Inge play on Broadway just a few years earlier, a mother advises her daughter that, "A pretty girl doesn't have long, just a few years. Then she's the equal of kings and she can walk out of a shanty... and live in a palace with a doting husband...." The movie version of *Picnic* came out in 1955 and probably illustrates what many at the time believed.

As commentators have suggested, maybe Grace Kelly simply wanted to make a grand exit while she was at the top. If Carroll Righter had advised her, he would have noted that Saturn would spend the next several years transiting the lower part of her chart, a period that Grant Lewi believed to be a time of professional obscurity. And Grace's natal Sun-Moon-Pluto grand trine also foreshadowed a major transformation in her life.

Grace was required to agree that their children would remain with the Prince and Monaco, no matter what happened. And she had to submit to a medical exam that proved she could conceive. These must have been tough issues to address, but with so many favorably aspected Scorpio planets in her chart, she was up to the challenge. Taurus on her seventh house of partnerships and contracts is ruled by beautiful Venus in Libra conjunct her Ascendant, so contracts in general could be favorable for her, including this very important marriage agreement. The ruler of the seventh both dignified and conjunct the Ascendant is also an astrological signature of a fortunate marriage coming right to her. Although with transiting Neptune conjunct her Venus at the time, she could easily have had illusions about this partnership.

Kelly remained under contract to MGM, who insisted on filming the wedding if it was to release her. The pair were married on April 18, 1956 in Monte Carlo. After the wedding, there was a reception for the citizens of Monaco and a gala at the opera house. A religious ceremony followed the next day, and the couple had to repeat the ceremony once again for the MGM cameras, a process Grace would later describe as a "nightmare." The resulting film was broadcast to 30 million viewers in nine countries. The Prince and Princess then left on a six-week honeymoon cruise.

A wedding chart represents the ceremony itself, but it can also be used to analyze the potential of the marriage astrologically. Uranus in Cancer rises, showing the phenomenal publicity that the wedding attracted. But the first house also indicates the person who initiated the union, often the man who proposes. The Ascendant is in Cancer with its ruler, the Moon in Leo, also in the first house. This seems to appropriately represent the Prince, who needed to continue his royal line.

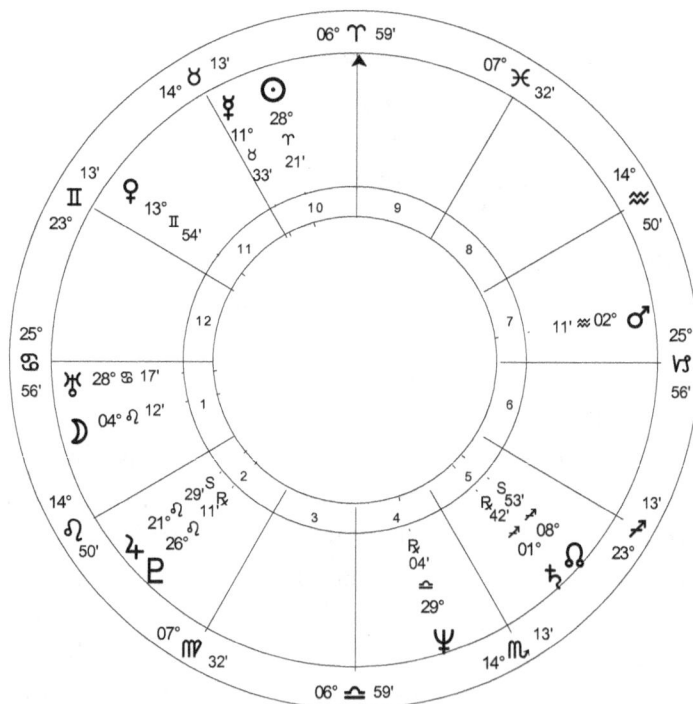

Grace Marries the Prince of Monaco
April 18, 1956, 11:10 a.m., Monte Carlo, Monaco.
Source: Astrologers Doris Chase Doane and Carol Peel in
A Time for Astrology cite time the ceremony was completed.

But the Moon conjunct Uranus is involved in a complicated grand cross, with both planets opposing Mars in Aquarius in the seventh house. These three planets all square the Sun in Aries in the tenth and Neptune in Libra in the fourth house, creating a volatile pattern.

The Sun in the prominent tenth house of position also represents the Prince (since it rules the first house Moon in Leo), and he seems to be at cross-purposes with himself, as the Sun squares both of the first house planets. He had the power and prestige to accomplish his goals (the Sun exalted in Aries), but may have been too radical in his actions (Uranus). Grace later found him to be fast-tempered, moody and strong-willed. And since the first house planets oppose Mars in the seventh, representing Grace, the two did not have much in common.

If we look at the wedding chart like a horary and make the seventh the first, we can see Grace's side of the equation. Capricorn is her first house, with Mars placed in Aquarius: she had taken a calculated risk with an offbeat choice. Mars, Grace's significator in the wedding chart, also reflects her own natal Mars, which is rising and configured with the Sun and Moon in her birth chart, too. Here, though, with its squares and oppositions, it presents more of a challenge.

Neptune in the turned tenth house also mirrors her own natal placement and suggests that she was deceived somehow, since it squares her significator Mars. Her romantic illusions had carried the day. Mars, also in square to the Sun in the turned fourth house, shows a new home that she'd have to fight for. She did not speak much French at first, and it took almost five years before the people of Monaco accepted her. And of course Mars opposing the Moon and Uranus could show her in conflict with an unpredictable partner. The Prince did not like Grace's Hollywood friends, and was soon spending time with mistresses.

But there are also some very nice aspects in the wedding horoscope. Jupiter conjoins Pluto in Leo in the second house, and both trine the Sun in the tenth and sextile Neptune, interfering with the Sun-Neptune opposition. The image of the principality was revived by the marriage, its economy improved, and their own sense of security grew as a result. Saturn in the fifth house of children trines the Moon and Uranus and sextiles Mars, interfering with the Moon and Uranus' oppositions to Mars. The couple's children, Caroline, born in 1957, Albert the following year, and Stephanie in 1965, must have given them a sense of comfort and security. Having a family seems to have been a goal that both of them shared, and Monaco needed an heir in order to remain independent.

Grace, though, was also rumored to have had an affair with Frank Sinatra after Caroline was born, and another affair with a friend's husband in New York a few years later. Though she could no longer act, she worked on behalf of the arts, children and mothers, and created intricate needlework pieces and collages of pressed flowers, all expressions of her fifth house Moon in Pisces. In 1962 the actor David Niven moved nearby, and they became good friends. (Born on March 1, 1910, he had the Sun in Pisces and the Moon in Scorpio, the reverse of Grace's natal placements, making them natural companions.)

While the Prince and Princess remained legally married, as the years went on they led increasingly independent lives, as might be expected from a wedding horoscope with an angular Uranus opposite Mars. The Princess often traveled alone, and finally moved to Paris with the children in 1976.

Grace's continued interest in astrology, psychics and séances throughout her life is clear from her prominent, metaphysically-inclined Scorpio planets, as well as Jupiter in her eighth house. She believed that she, herself, had ESP, which also seems possible. She was said to have had a premonition that she'd die in a car crash, something Carroll Righter may have also suspected from her eighth house Jupiter in Gemini, which relates to travel. Since natal Jupiter sextiled Uranus, we could also guess that her end might be sudden or unexpected. Driving 17-year-old Stephanie home on the morning of September 13, 1982, Grace suffered a stroke, and her car skidded off the road and crashed. She was not yet 53 years old and died of her injuries the following day.

The public continues to be fascinated by the enigmatic young Scorpio woman who was captured for posterity in all those classic films of the 1950s. And just like the movies that preserve her youthful appeal, we can still turn to her horoscope to see what she was really like.

Notes and Sources:

Inge, William, *Four Plays by William Inge*. Random House, New York, 1958.

Lacey, Robert, *Grace Kelly*. G.P. Putnam's Sons, New York, 1994.

Leigh, Wendy, *True Grace*. St. Martin's Press, New York, 2007.

Lewi, Grant, *Astrology for the Millions*. Doubleday, Doran & Co., New York, 1940.

Stearn, Jess, *A Time for Astrology*. Signet Books, New York, 1971.

Hope Cooke and the King of Sikkim

Can astrologers evade destiny with electional charts? American Hope Cooke was famous in the 1960s as the Queen of Sikkim. Her birth chart indicates her dysfunctional family background, her high-powered marriage and the tumultuous political situations she encountered. Her synastry with her husband and the transits they shared all show similar dynamics. But their wedding chart, elected by Tibetan astrologers, could not overcome the obstacles of birth charts, compatibility and transits.

Hope Cooke was born on June 24, 1940. She had many emotional upheavals as a girl: her parents divorced and her mother, an amateur pilot, died in a plane crash when she was just two. Hope and her half-sister were raised by their grandparents. Their grandfather was a wealthy shipping executive, and the girls attended exclusive schools in New York City. Hope's grandparents died when she was a teenager, and she went to live with her aunt and uncle, a U.S. Ambassador in Iran.

Hope's early limitations and loss seem to be due to restrictive Capricorn on her fourth house cusp of home and family, ruled by Saturn conjunct her eighth house cusp. Saturn-like, her grandparents were her most important parental figures, but they were not warm people. Hope and her sister were actually raised by an elderly nanny in a separate apartment.

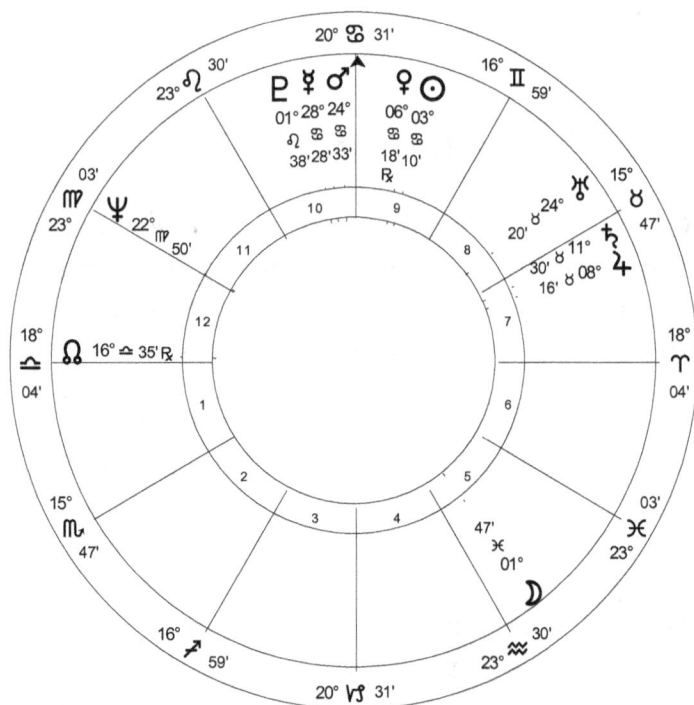

Hope Cooke
June 24, 1940, 1:27 p.m., San Francisco, California.
Source: Birth Certificate and *Astrodatabank.*

The Moon in Pisces shows Hope's sensitive feelings and her adaptable emotional nature, but its exact quincunx to Pluto also indicates the trauma she experienced in her family; this signature seems in keeping with being a "poor little rich girl." The Moon also forms an out-of-sign square to Uranus in the eighth house, pointing towards some tumultuous changes in her home and family; it's also a potent symbol for her absentee aviatrix mother as well.

Under her aunt and uncle's influence, Hope did much international traveling, and was attracted to the East. Her Sun in Cancer falls in the ninth house of long-distance travel, along with Venus, the ruler of her Libra Ascendant, creating one of the most positive outlets in her horoscope. It seems like Hope was happiest in Iran. She later attended Sarah Lawrence College in New York, majored in Asian studies, and continued to travel on holidays. After a long trip to Russia with friends in the summer of 1959, she settled into the Windermere Hotel in Darjeeling, India, to teach herself typing and economics. While there, she was introduced to the Crown Prince of Sikkim.

Sikkim, about the size of the state of Delaware, was already a protectorate of its neighbor, India, but retained some independence under the Chogyal, or King. Sikkim was part of the Himalayan region best known to people in the west as the mythic city of Shangri-La in books and movies. Its actual landscape was dramatic: valleys of subtropical foliage starkly contrasting with towering mountains covered with snow. Rising out of this incredible vista of sacred peaks and mystic lakes is the dramatic Mt. Kanchenjunga, the "Great Snow Mountain of the Five Treasures," the third tallest mountain in the world. (The magician and occultist Aleister Crowley, a skilled mountain climber, attempted to climb Kanchenjunga in 1905, and a British team finally reached the summit in 1955.) Heinrich Hasser's *Seven Years in Tibet* had come out in 1953, giving the public one of its first glimpses into this mysterious and isolated part of the world. When the Dalai Lama fled Tibet for India to escape Chinese Communists in 1959, the Himalayas continued to be associated with spirituality and the Buddhist concepts of repeated birth, death and reincarnation.

Palden Thondup Namgyal, the Maharaj Kumar, was a widower with two sons and a daughter who was studying in Darjeeling, bringing him to the city where he met Hope. Palden was born on May 23, 1923. His Sun, Mercury and Mars were in charismatic and changeable Gemini, making him intelligent and multi-lingual. He was believed to be the reincarnation of a Buddhist priest and had studied to become a monk as a youngster. These issues are suggested by his Jupiter in Scorpio, the sign most often associated with reincarnation, in a grand trine involving Uranus, the "awakener," and Pluto, the planet we connect with past lives.

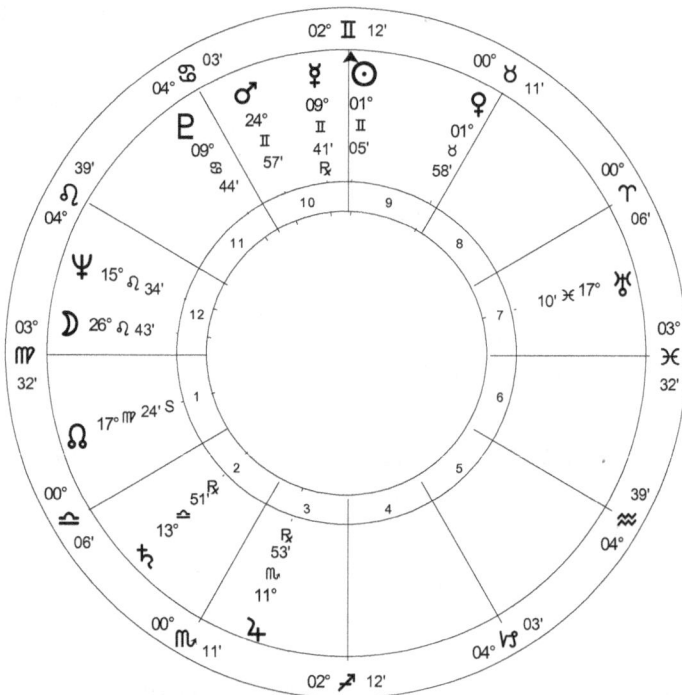

Palden Thondup Namgyal

May 23, 1923, Gangtok, Sikkim (now India); noon chart.
Source: *Wikipedia*.com. Some sources list May 22, 1923, but this does not change the planets much (still a Leo Moon).

Palden's older brother's death in a plane crash completely changed his life as he then became the Crown Prince and was educated in India. Pluto's square to Saturn in Libra in Palden's chart may suggest he had a more significant mission in the material world (Saturn) and with relationships and diplomacy (Libra).

After India became independent of Great Britain, the Maharaj Kumar headed up the negotiating team that hammered out Sikkim's relationship with India. He married in 1950, but his first wife died just seven years later. After he met Hope in Darjeeling in the summer of 1959, she visited his palace several times. He was 36 and she was just 19. Hope returned to school in the fall and the two didn't reconnect for another few years — when Hope was invited to Sikkim on several occasions to meet Palden's family. The couple announced their engagement on Christmas Day, 1961.

These two people made a commitment to one other at unusual turning points in their lives. Transiting Uranus in Virgo stationed in square to Palden's Gemini Sun at the time, bringing a unique development to his life. Transiting Pluto in Virgo was also in a close square to his Mercury in Gemini, making for a tough and possibly fateful decision. Transiting Neptune in Scorpio was activating his grand water trine and had just conjoined his natal Jupiter; he may have been unconsciously drawn to the wealthy foreigner.

Transiting Saturn in Capricorn opposed Hope's tenth house Mercury, bringing her notoriety and changing her status. Transiting Uranus, often the harbinger of the radically new and different, stationed in close opposition to her Pisces Moon, and she had made a life-altering choice. Transiting Pluto stationing at 10°

Virgo was very close to trining Hope's Jupiter-Saturn midpoint. If we see the Crown Prince's natal Jupiter-Pluto and Saturn-Pluto combinations as somehow karmic, Hope's transit involving all three of these planets has similar resonances.

We need to examine Hope Cooke's seventh house of partnerships, along with planets placed in and ruling the seventh to analyze her astrological options for marriage. Hope has Jupiter in the seventh house, generally considered an excellent placement, giving luck through marriage. Her marriage also gave her a lot of publicity. Since Jupiter also rules both foreigners and people in high places, its influence in Cooke's life is clear, especially since Jupiter also favorably sextiles both her Sun and Venus in her ninth house. But Jupiter is also closely conjunct Saturn, toning down its expansive energies. And since Saturn is only about four degrees from the Placidus eighth house cusp, many astrologers would consider its influence, at least in part, to work for the eighth.

Saturn in the eighth house gives us people with a strong sense of responsibility in close relationships. With Taurus, the sign of wealth, on the eighth, the house associated with legacies, Hope had inherited a significant amount of money from her grandparents. But her marriage would come with the obligations and the responsibilities of royalty and the limitations of Saturn.

Aries on her seventh house has its ruler Mars conjunct the Midheaven (the ruler of the seventh house placed in the tenth), showing that Hope's partner could improve her status. But since Mars is in water sign Cancer, it could also raise some emotional issues. Though Mars is well aspected with sextiles to the outer planets Uranus and Neptune, Uranus' placement in the eighth house and Neptune's conjunct the twelfth both lend complexity and complications to her relationships through their connections with Mars.

We can see the attraction Hope and the Maharaj Kumar had for one another, as there are many classic aspects involving Venus and Mars in their synastry, giving them sexual chemistry and compatibility. His Venus in Taurus fell in her seventh house, conjoining her Jupiter and sextiling her Sun, Moon and Venus, showing easily shared feelings and an open attraction. His Mars conjoined her Sun, adding a sexual spark. Her ruler, Venus, trined his Jupiter, and her Mars trined his Uranus, signifying a nice give and take. They could introduce each other to new and stimulating experiences. Her Sun and Venus also conjoined his Pluto, an intense aspect of attraction, but one that might also present complications. This relationship was certainly deeper than simple Venus-Mars attraction.

Since Sikkim was an Asian country bordering India, Tibet, Nepal and Bhutan, astrology was part of the fabric of its life. The Tibetan court astrologer had actually selected the Crown Prince's engagement date, the same one chosen for his sister's wedding, but also decreed that 1962 was unfortunate for marriage. Tibet is now part of China, another one of its closest neighbors, and Tibetan astrology shows both Chinese and Indian influences. 1962 was a Tiger year in Chinese astrology, creating an unpredictable and turbulent time (Hope later recalled that there were floods in Sikkim and the Chinese attacked the Indian border in 1962). And since the Tiger is said to be an enemy of hierarchy, it was not the best choice for a royal marriage. 1963, a Hare (or Rabbit) year, had a more peaceful, calm and prudent influence. The astrologers scheduled the wedding for 1963, and Hope returned to New York to finish her college education.

Saturn can typically bring delay as well as important life developments, and both individuals' lives were affected by Saturn's transit at the same time (similar chart degrees can show shared experiences as a transit hits both charts). Saturn had moved into Aquarius in 1962, squaring Hope's seventh house Jupiter in Taurus from her fourth, so she was in the midst of change from her old life (her fourth house home in New York) to the new (a foreign marriage; Jupiter in her seventh house). Transiting Saturn trined the Prince's Sun, Mercury and Saturn, creating a grand trine in air signs, so the transition must have been somewhat easier for him. Yet Saturn also squared his Jupiter in Scorpio, too, causing a frustrating delay for him as well. The couple's natal Jupiter opposite Jupiter is an obvious signifier of their cultural, religious and ethnic differences, and transiting Saturn represented the astrological authorities who insisted upon waiting.

But delay is often not a bad thing for a relationship, as Saturn, considered exalted in Libra, teaches us. Couples may share marvelous Venus and Mars aspects, giving them attraction, but lack connections that make for long-term cooperation, something that's essential for marriage. Over time, when the initial attraction and excitement ruled by Venus and Mars has worn off, these things reveal themselves more clearly.

Saturn connections between two horoscopes often describe how the couple collaborates over time, and whether they're constructive, responsible and willing to work at the relationship. Hope's Saturn closely opposed

Palden's Jupiter and squared his Neptune. While she could have been dedicated to understanding him, he may have foiled her efforts. Compromise would be necessary. His Saturn had no close major aspects to any of Hope's planets, but it did conjoin her Ascendant and North Node. These are aspects of permanence, with the Prince figuratively "holding onto" Hope. He represented her eighth house Saturn, someone who would provide some stability. He was also seventeen years older and more experienced in life. But there is certainly nothing romantic about Saturn, especially on one's Ascendant.

Hope's aunt and uncle were relieved to hear that the Maharaj Kumar already had two male heirs—sparing their niece any pressure or anxiety about having a family right away, as many royal wives are pressed to do. But there were other limitations to the relationship that Hope may not have shared with her family. Palden had a mistress, a woman he seemed to be involved with when they first got to know one another, and he and Hope argued about her continued presence in his life. Their dynamic inter-aspects involving the Sun, Mars and Pluto may illuminate this issue as they seem to describe a contest of wills.

Why would Hope marry someone who was already having an affair? Let's remember that she was young, just 22, when she married. Most people aren't fully aware of their own strengths and weaknesses at that age (which is probably more likely after the first Saturn return). As her ninth house planets suggest, Hope was extraordinarily drawn to the East. She had never had a real Cancerian home, and she must have felt a connection with Sikkim, an exotic land that nicely draws on the Cancer and ninth house energies in her chart. Her horoscope has much water, not known to make logical decisions, especially in matters of the heart. Her relationship houses (the seventh and eighth) hold planets in Taurus, a fixed sign craving permanence. And she probably wanted children: both her Sun and Venus in maternal Cancer are trine the Moon in Pisces in her fifth house.

The wedding was on with a date selected by the court astrologers, which was March 20, 1963 in Gangtok (now part of India). The royal wedding party was dressed in silk brocade and gold and accompanied by kilted bagpipers, a remnant of the days of British conquest. Ten-foot trumpets announced the start of the Buddhist ceremony with foghorn-like blasts beginning at around 9:00 a.m., and the marriage was sealed with an exchange of silk scarves, the Tibetan equivalent of "I do," at around 10:00. We'll use this 10:00 a.m. time as the chart for the wedding, which had the Sun conjunct Jupiter in Pisces. The marriage received worldwide media attention and was covered in the *Saturday Evening Post*, *Vogue* and *National Geographic*, among many other publications. Hope was now the Maharaj Kumarani. Guests came from many countries, and included an American Ambassador, Buddhist monks, Indian Maharajas, Sikkimese, Tibetans and westerners. Tibetan and Nepalese folk dancers in colorful costumes welcomed the couple as they left the temple.

The Maharaja of neighboring Bhutan, age 35, also attended the wedding. He suffered a heart attack at the reception, which some might have seen as an ill omen for the marriage. But since he'd already had his first heart attack fifteen years earlier and had health challenges throughout his life, this traumatic event may not have seemed as unusual at the time as it now appears.

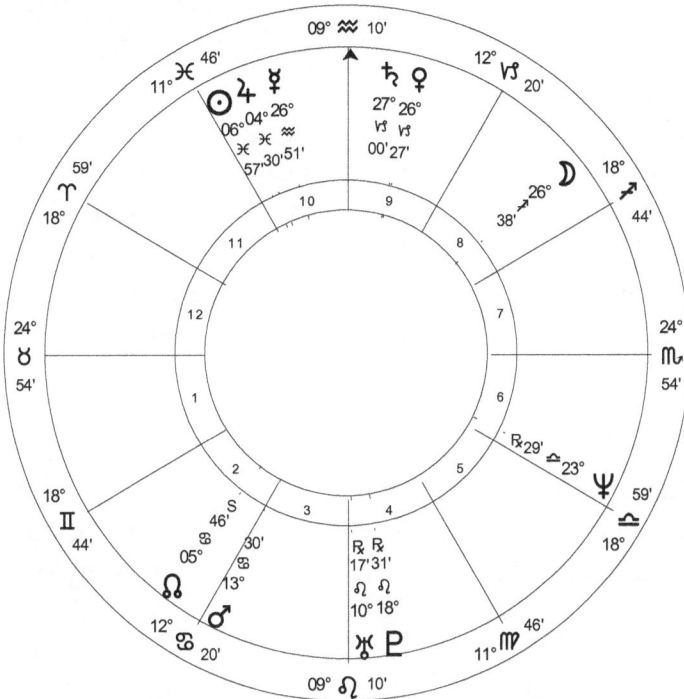

Hope Cooke Marries the Maharaj Kumar
March 20, 1963, 10:00 a.m., Gangtok, India;
Sidereal. Source: *Saturday Evening Post*, May 11, 1963.

Since Tibetan and Indian astrology have some similarities to their Western counterpart, we can get an idea of what the royal astrologers might have been looking for in their electional chart. In the wedding horoscope, there are conjunctions and sextiles between the Moon, Mercury and Jupiter, and a trine between Venus conjunct Saturn and the Ascendant. These are mostly favorable. But India typically utilizes the Sidereal zodiac, based on the constellations (our western zodiac is based on the seasons). The ayanamsha, or distance between our Tropical zodiac and the Tibetan one at the time was about 22°. If we subtract 22° from all the placements in our usual Western horoscope, we'll have a better picture of what the Sidereal astrologers liked about this chart.

One of the things both Indian and Western astrology share is the concept of essential dignity. Jupiter is in one of its traditional ruling signs, Pisces, in both the Tropical and Sidereal wedding charts. Saturn is in its ruling sign of Capricorn in the Sidereal zodiac and coincidentally it falls in its other ruling sign of Aquarius in our Western zodiac.

The Moon is in sidereal Sagittarius, a lively sign representing expansion and intercultural relations, ruled by lucky Jupiter. One can't have everything in any marriage election, and the Tibetan astrologers had many additional variables to juggle. However they do not typically use the outer planets. A Western astrologer may not have chosen Uranus conjunct the IC, which might foreshadow instability in the home, or Neptune squaring both Venus and Saturn, highlighting Hope's Saturn square Palden's Neptune in their compatibility. Some Sikkimese objected to the extravagance of the wedding and the four-day festivities, which 5,000 were invited to attend.

Transiting Uranus was sextiling Hope's Sun, and transiting Pluto trined Hope's eighth house Saturn at the time. Since both the Sun and Saturn show important men in one's life, there was a significant development, and she got married. But her uncle also died just four days after the wedding, which he'd been unable to attend due to illness. Then, on December 2, 1963, less than a year later, the elderly King of Sikkim died. Hope had barely had time to get used to her new life before this significant event. The astrologers also played a role in death, and decided how long the King's coffin should be kept in the royal chapel, as well as when the body would be cremated. The Maharaj Kumar now became the twelfth Chogyal (or King) of Sikkim.

With the Sun and Venus in Cancer trining her fifth house Moon, Hope Cooke, now Gyalmo (or Queen) of Sikkim, had a tremendous capacity for love, and found an outlet in her children. Prince Palden (Jr.) was born on February 20, 1964 and Princess Hope Leezum was born in 1968. In her book, *Time Changes*, Hope speaks of happy times with her children and stepchildren. But there were difficulties with her marriage; no wedding chart can eliminate a couple's synastry. Like other royal brides, Hope was lonely, she didn't speak the local languages, and she found it hard to make friends. The Chogyal was often busy, and he seemed to keep up with his mistresses. Hope felt resentment from her sister-in-law, who lived with them, and her American background became an issue in the complex political situation in Sikkim. Over time, though, Hope acclimated herself, learning Sikkimese and teaching at a local school, both excellent outlets for her fifth and ninth house planets relating to young people and education. As she became more mature and experienced, she seemed to be utilizing the promise of her horoscope in a more positive way.

The astrologers might have foreseen, but were unable to prevent the changes in the country that followed. Sikkim was made up of many ethnic groups, and nearly three-quarters of the population were immigrants from Nepal who had won citizenship in

1961; they agitated in 1972 to demand better representation. This led to activism for democratic reforms, civil unrest and riots before the palace, resulting in a request for help from India. The Chogyal was placed under house arrest in April of 1973, and Hope considered themselves "incarcerated" for nearly two months. It had become dangerous to be part of the royal family, and on August 15, 1973, after ten years as Queen, Hope Cooke returned to New York with her children.

Uranus conjunct the fourth house of the wedding chart certainly seems an apt symbol for the chaotic upheaval that ended this unusual relationship. At the time of the siege and her departure, transiting Uranus in Libra also conjoined Hope's first house cusp and squared her Midheaven, accurately describing the sudden events that occurred, as well as her increased independence. Sikkim became part of India in 1975, and the Chogyal was deposed. Hope and Palden remained separated and were divorced in 1980, when Hope's autobiography was published. The Chogyal died of cancer in January of 1982, shortly after his second Saturn return.

Hope and her children remained in New York. The ninth house also indicates second marriages (as it's the third, or a multiple, of the seventh). And Hope's Sun conjunct Venus trining the Moon in the fifth certainly describes a warmer, more loving union. In 1999 she married a history professor and Pulitzer Prize winning author, although this marriage, too, eventually ended in divorce. Hope further maximized her ninth house Sun and Venus in Cancer, giving walking tours of New York City, and wrote a book about them while living quietly in an old brownstone in Brooklyn.

Notes and Sources:

Battaglia, Lee E., "Wedding of Two Worlds," *National Geographic*, Volume 124, November, 1963.

Cooke, Hope, *Time Change*, Simon & Schuster, New York, 1980.

Cornu, Philippe, *Tibetan Astrology*, Shambhala Publications, Boston and London, 1997.

Ross, Nancy Wilson, "A Royal Princess," *Saturday Evening Post*, May 11, 1963.

Wikipedia.org profiles of Hope Cooke and Palden Thondup Namgyal.

Lisa Halaby and the King of Jordan

Although Lisa Halaby was a child of privilege who grew up in New York City, California and Washington D.C., she could never have imagined that she'd one day become the Queen of Jordan.

Her father, once the president of Pan American Airlines, also worked for the State Department and the Pentagon. Lisa's grandfather had come to the U.S. from Syria as a boy. Her blonde hair and blue eyes were from her mother, who was Swedish, although Lisa is a quarter Arab. The eldest of three children, she often felt shy and was a loner with poor eyesight as a girl. She nevertheless had a strong independent streak, loved horses and nature and later excelled in sports. She went on to be part of the first co-ed class at Princeton University, and earned an architecture degree in 1974 after taking a year off in Aspen, Colorado, where she worked as a maid and waitress and studied photography.

Halaby was born on August 23, 1951 in Washington D.C. This date is right on the cusp of Leo and Virgo. Lisa would most likely be Leo, with a Leo Sun sign during most of that day; she would have the Sun in Virgo if she were born after 7:30 p.m. Unfortunately, no birth time has ever been published for her. To further complicate things, she also has Mercury and Venus conjoined in Virgo, and Mars and Pluto both in Leo, so she would have characteristics of both signs in any case. Friends at college described her as "determined" and "controlled," which sound more like fixed sign Leo. Lisa, herself, says she is a Leo in her autobiography, *Leap of Faith* (on page 315). And she did become a queen!

Even with Mercury and Venus in Virgo, what Leo could work as a maid, describe herself as a "dedicated minimalist" and admit to feeling uncomfortable wearing jewelry? I have therefore speculated that she has the Sun in the twelfth house, which would tone down her Leo characteristics and accentuate the Virgo, giving her Virgo rising with Venus conjunct the Ascendant and Saturn also in the first house.

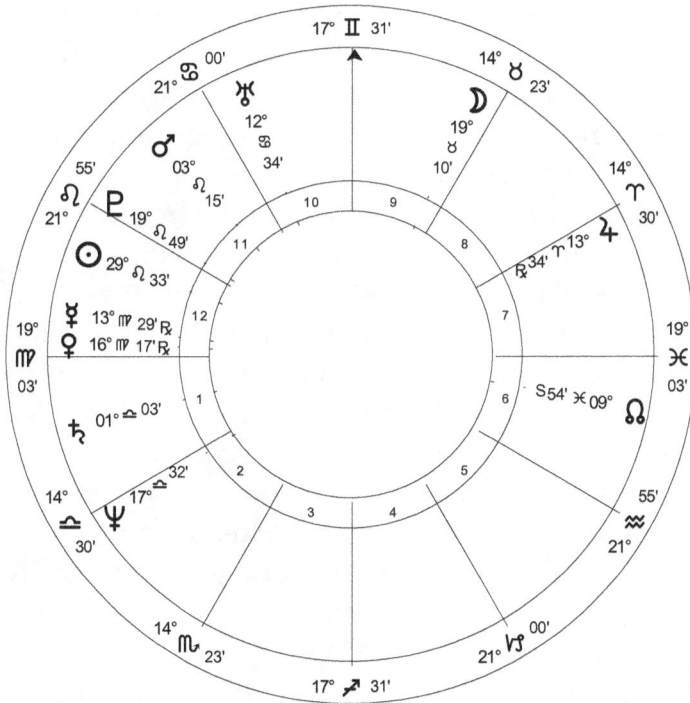

Lisa Halaby
August 23, 1951, Washington D.C.; time is speculative.
Source: *Biography.com* and many other sources.

Halaby's horoscope presents a classic combination of challenging and flowing aspects. A T-square of Jupiter,

Uranus and Neptune presents high ideals and an unsettled nature. Her Jupiter in Aries may have contributed to the many moves in her childhood, but as a young adult she also travelled widely. After college, she worked for an architectural firm in Sydney, Australia, and as a planning assistant for a city center in Iran.

A little later, an assignment with her father's aviation firm brought her to Jordan. King Hussein was an enthusiastic aviator himself, and Halaby met him briefly on several occasions. On April 7, 1977, her father was in Jordan as a consultant for Alia Airlines and brought her to a meeting with the King. They soon found common interests and began seeing one another, and the King proposed marriage in about a month.

Lisa tells us in her memoirs that she immediately felt at home when she first came to Jordan, and began studying Arabic. With the Moon in Taurus, the sign of its exaltation, her feelings were strong, and with its trines to Mercury and Venus in Virgo, she would gravitate toward those things that made her feel comfortable and secure. She found King Hussein easy to talk to and was never conscious of their fifteen-year age difference (she was 26 and he 41). She accepted Hussein's proposal on May 13, 1977. What was happening astrologically to create such a whirlwind of events?

Just before Lisa's meeting with the King, a lunar eclipse on April 4 at 14° Libra conjoined transiting Pluto, and both activated her significant T-square. Whatever one can say about a challenging T-square pattern, it often portends well-timed events when activated. Transiting Uranus, the harbinger of surprises, was in Scorpio and exactly trined Lisa's North Node by the end of the month. It was also trining her natal Uranus as well, ushering in exciting events as it created a grand trine in her chart. A solar eclipse also closely trined her Sun on April 18. And in June, while solidifying plans for her marriage the following year, transiting Saturn in Leo trined her natal Jupiter, representing both settling down (Saturn's influence) as well as her further expansion into a far-off land (her natal Jupiter's potential).

At the time they met, King Hussein was a widower with eight children. He was a Hashemite, known as direct descendants of the Prophet Muhammad, and both Shi'ites and Sunni viewed the Hashemites as spiritual leaders. Jordan is also strategically located between Israel, Saudi Arabia, Syria and Iraq, with neighbors Egypt and Lebanon not far away. Hussein was in an unusual position and worked for Arab unity and peace, a voice of moderation in the often turbulent Middle East political scene.

King Hussein was born on November 14, 1935 and had a remarkable horoscope with a number of notable features. A kite pattern gave ease of success in some areas of life. Made up of a grand trine in water signs between the Moon in Cancer conjoined with his Midheaven and trines to Mercury in Scorpio and Saturn in Pisces, we can see his family prominence and deep feelings about his country (the Moon in Cancer) along with a responsible nature (Saturn) and realistic outlook (Mercury). Uranus provided one of the focal points for the kite, as it sextiled the Moon and Saturn and opposed Mercury. Uranus' influence made the King a life-long aviator who also loved ham radio and cars. Since Uranus was placed in his eighth house, it also contributed to instability in some of his closest connections, which included not only four marriages but dramatic experiences in his youth as well.

Hussein had the Sun in Scorpio in his second house, an obvious indicator of his tremendous inheritance. The Sun is somewhat widely conjoined with Jupiter in Sagittarius conjunct his third house cusp, and he enjoyed an international reputation. But the Sun and Jupiter also trine Pluto in the tenth house which, along with the complex sign of Scorpio, may have added to the upheavals in his life.

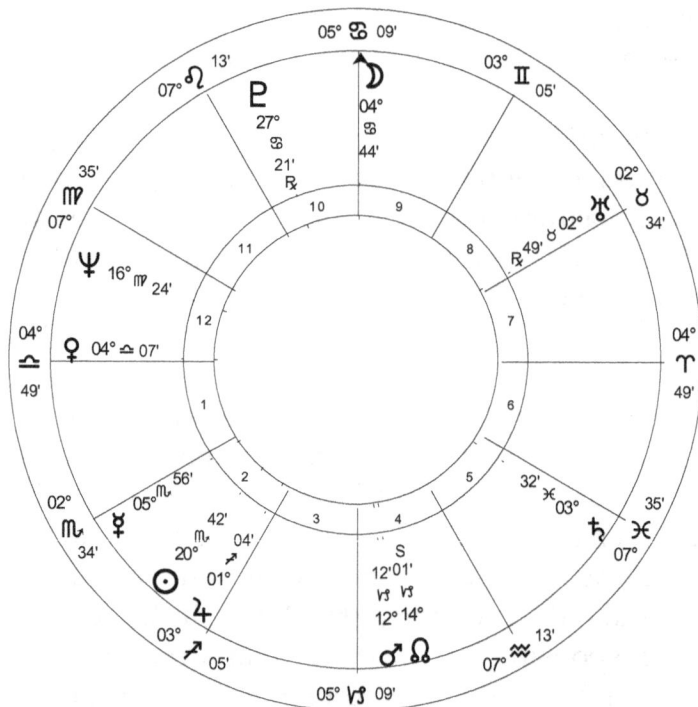

King Hussein of Jordan
November 14, 1935, 2:30 a.m., Amman, Jordan.
Source: Marc Penfield in *Mercury Hour*, April 1979,
cites an official time; see *Astrodatabank.com*.

Hussein bin Talal was born before Jordan became an independent state in 1949. He was not yet sixteen and accompanying his grandfather, King Abdullah, when he was assassinated by a Palestinian militant as they left a Jerusalem mosque. The following year his father (the current King), was removed by Parliament as unfit to rule (he is said to have suffered from schizophrenia). Hussein himself was crowned in 1953, six months before he turned eighteen. Although a flowing aspect, the Sun in Scorpio trine Pluto could nevertheless indicate some complicated issues surrounding power and authority figures. The political situation with Jordan's neighbors was often complex, and included the 1967 Arab-Israeli war when hundreds of thousands of refugees swept into Jordan. In 1970 the PLO tried to take control.

King Hussein's horoscope gives us an unusual example of angular planets and essential dignity, two of the most important characteristics that increase planetary power. His Moon in Cancer, its own sign, closely conjoined the Midheaven. His Venus in Libra, its own sign, closely conjoined the Ascendant, very apt symbolism for someone remembered as a peacemaker. And his Mars in Capricorn, the sign of its exaltation, fell in his fourth house, further symbolizing not only his powerful connection with his ancestry, but also the very real challenges his father and grandfather had faced. The Moon and Mars are both placed Out of Bounds in declination and are closely contraparallel, making their influence more extreme. And the Moon, Venus and Mars also form a T-square pattern, further energizing these already powerful planets and creating dynamic situations involving the King himself, his family, his country and his reputation.

Quincunx aspects (150°, also sometimes called inconjunct aspects) are ones of incongruity, and give a need for adjustments in life. The *Larousse Encyclopedia of Astrology* describes a double quincunx as giving a "strange and unusual destiny." Some also call this pattern a yod, and it's made up of at least three planets: a fulcrum planet with two quincunxes. The two planets on the far side of the pattern then sextile one another. The yod is also sometimes called a "Finger of God," interesting in light of Hussein's royal birth and the Hashemites descent from Muhammad. One of the most unusual things about King Hussein's horoscope are two double quincunx patterns, which intersect one another. Uranus in Taurus in the eighth house is inconjunct both Venus on the Ascendant and Jupiter in Sagittarius on the third house cusp; then Venus sextiles Jupiter. Al H. Morrison defined a true yod as including the heaviest planet at the apex point, and here Uranus is in that position. Morrison believed that this pattern made for someone with no internal confusion or conflict, as the energies of the faster-moving planets are funneled into the heavier one.

But Venus inconjunct Uranus is also part of another, intersecting, yod with Venus also quincunx Saturn. Saturn then sextiles Uranus. Morrison felt that this pattern, with a faster-moving planet at the apex (in this example, Venus), made for someone who was divided within himself. In Al's definition, this pattern would simply be called a double quincunx. With an intersecting yod and double quincunx, we have someone with both certainty and doubts. The King's unusual life and unique position in the Arab world seems reflected in these dynamic patterns.

If we consider Hussein's houses, we can interpret his experiences with his four marriages. (This kind of analysis may not always be the most accurate, but in Hussein's case appears appropriate.) His first marriage is related to his seventh house with Aries on its cusp, ruled by Mars in Capricorn in his fourth house. This marriage was arranged by his mother and short-lived: Hussein was only nineteen and his wife a distant cousin born in Egypt; they had one daughter. The second marriage is indicated by his ninth house and Gemini. Ruled by Mercury, part of his grand water trine with the Moon, Midheaven and Saturn, this marriage must have given him a sense of security and aided his reputation and status; he had two sons and twin daughters. Yet Mercury is also opposed to Uranus as part of the kite: this was an unusual match (she was the daughter of a British military officer), and it had the potential to break up.

The third marriage was a love match and is shown by Leo on the eleventh house, ruled by the Sun in Scorpio in the second conjoining Jupiter and trining Pluto. Hussein was deeply attached to Queen Alia, who was very popular in Jordan, and they had two children and adopted a baby girl. But she was tragically killed in a helicopter crash in early 1977. The intense feelings and life and death situations that may be experienced with important Scorpio and Pluto placements are obvious in this marriage. Jupiter's international influence can also be seen, since Alia was the Palestinian daughter of a diplomat. She had travelled the world and studied in the U.S.

Lisa, Hussein's fourth wife, is represented by his first house and Venus in Libra. This suggests that she was a true partner to him. And while Venus sextiles Jupiter, showing luck and once again the possibility of an international theme, Venus is also at the point of the yod involving Uranus and Saturn, which add heavier notes.

When they married, commentators were surprised that Lisa would be named a Queen and that she had converted to Islam. She tells us in her autobiography that the Arabic name the King gave her, Queen Noor al Hussein, which means "Light of Hussein," transformed her. With the Sun in Leo, she could easily be a light in his life, and her Sun is somewhat widely conjunct Pluto, the sign of transformation. Pluto also squares the Moon, trines Jupiter and sextiles Neptune in Lisa's natal chart (Jupiter is opposite Neptune in her T-square). So transformation would be important in her life and could also feel positive and natural to her.

Lisa did not have a strong religious background, although she'd been raised as a Christian Scientist. She'd felt drawn toward Islam since arriving in the Middle East. She now had a sense of belonging to a larger community for the first time.

A T-square generates intense energies that may not be easily channeled. In Lisa's case, with Uranus as the focal point with squares to Jupiter and Neptune, she is quite a unique and idealistic individual, but may not have known exactly what to do with these urges when young. It can certainly be said that transcendental planets like Uranus and Neptune are easier to manage as we mature and have more experience of life.

Before Lisa came to Jordan at the age of 26, she had travelled widely, enjoyed athletic interests and had several short-term professional positions. It appears that she had been restless, without an overriding focus for her energies, a seeker of something ineffable. As she accepted the King's proposal and her new identity, she not only drew upon the transformative power of Pluto, but also found an ideal outlet for her spiritual values (Jupiter), community spirit (Uranus) and compassion (Neptune). Her dynamic Jupiter in Aries also helped her connect with her Arab heritage in quite an unusual manner. And her new life in Jordan would be a tremendous adventure as well.

With both Mercury and Venus in Virgo, Halaby is service-oriented and needed a purpose in life. With her marriage, she found a major one. Her strong Moon in Taurus enjoyed a new home and her Leo Sun gained expression in a very visible position. She embraced her role as step-mother to eight children, three of whom lived with them.

Lisa had proclaimed the testimony of faith in Islam a few days before the wedding, which was on June 15, 1978. The marriage ceremony was simple and brief, taking place in a small, ornate Arabesque room at the Zaharan Palace. Lisa wore a white silk Dior gown and was the only woman present, according to Muslim custom. The couple sat next to each other on a couch and signed the marriage contract, with Lisa writing right to left in Arabic. Some verses were read from the Koran as they exchanged brief Arabic vows, clasped hands, looked at one another and joined the reception in the next room.

Queen Noor and King Hussein shared good aspects for compatibility. With fixed signs in their charts, they were both committed and determined. Scorpio might not seem the natural partner for a Leo (she tells us that he was a night, and she, a day person), but a Scorpio knows he can trust an open, heartfelt Leo, and a Leo will not be overly disturbed by the sometimes tortured nature of Scorpio. Her Sun sextiled his Moon in Cancer, and his Mars in Capricorn completed a grand trine in earth signs with her Moon in Taurus and Mercury and Venus in Virgo. With flowing lunar aspects, they could live together comfortably. In addition to his Mars in Capricorn trining her Venus in Virgo, his Venus rising in Libra closely sextiled her Mars in Leo, traditionally favorable aspects for sexual chemistry. She must have indeed been a light in his life.

Their inter-cultural connection is symbolized by Hussein's Jupiter in Sagittarius closely squaring Noor's Sun and exactly sextiling her Saturn. He expanded her outlook through the square aspect, but in ways which were also comfortable and long-lasting, symbolized by the sextile. Her Jupiter in Aries squared his Mars in Capricorn; while they may have had differences, it once again appears that she provided a lively antidote to his serious nature.

Saturn, of course, is almost always evident in the compatibility of long-term couples, and this relationship lasted more than twenty years. His Saturn opposed her Sun and her Saturn conjoined his Venus and Ascendant. Saturn conjunct someone else's Ascendant may show them finding a sense of stability and purpose with the other person. With Hussein's Saturn opposite Noor's Sun, he brought position, status, duties and a great amount of responsibility to her. Given the circumstances of their lives, this seems appropriate. In many ways their relationship would never be a care-free one; there were Saturnian limitations from the beginning. Hussein was a significant authority figure and Lisa would not have the freedom she had experienced before her marriage. But with transiting Saturn conjoining her Sun at the time of the wedding, she willingly entered into this significant commitment.

The wedding chart has Uranus rising in Scorpio trine Jupiter in Cancer. This shows their uncommon connection but also celebrates cultural tradition since Jupiter is in the sign of its exaltation (there are aspects between these two planets in each of their individual birth charts as well). Jupiter in Cancer also seems appropriate for Lisa's marriage into a large, ready-made family. The Sun and Mercury in Gemini may show the interests that the couple shared and perhaps also a clear-headedness in their decision to marry; though not totally clear, since the wedding Sun also opposes idealistic and deceptive Neptune.

The transiting North Node was stationary at 2° Libra, conjoining both Hussein's Ascendant and Lisa's Saturn, and ushering both into a new cycle of life experience.

While there are not many aspects in this wedding horoscope, the Moon in Libra trines the Gemini Sun but also conjoins Pluto, an aspect that would exist no matter what time of day the couple married. This may suggest the complexities of Lisa's many new step-children and their mothers, as well as the often tumultuous Middle East political situation that encroached on the couple's domestic life (though Lisa's natal Moon square Pluto would have helped her handle these kinds of issues). Mars in Virgo conjunct Saturn in Leo indicates the need for time, patience and dedication in order to avoid frustrations. This signature may also be responsible for the brevity and simplicity of the wedding ceremony.

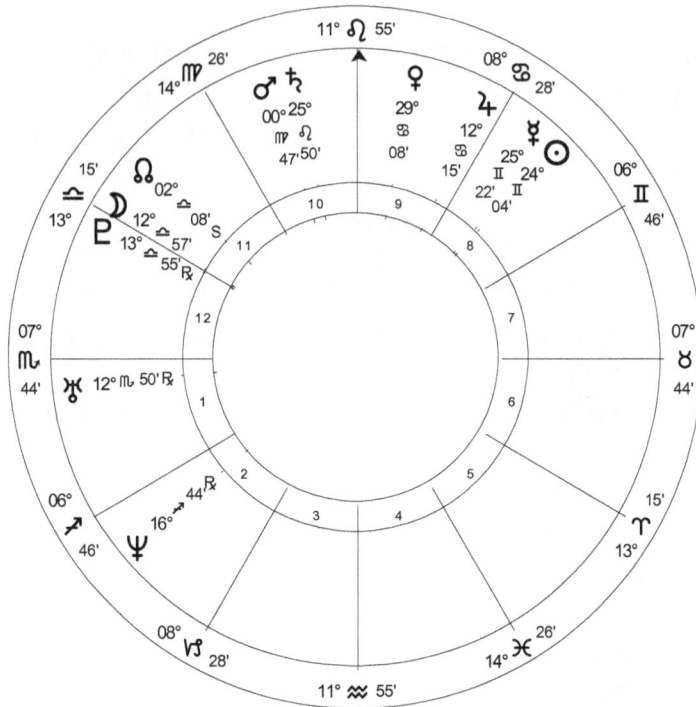

Lisa Marries the King of Jordan
June 15, 1978, Amman, Jordan; about 4:00 p.m.
Source: The *New York Times* quoted a Jordanian evening
news broadcast "a few hours after the quiet wedding."

Queen Noor found the lack of privacy in her new life a challenge. She was surrounded by servants and followed by bodyguards. The King did not give her much guidance and was often away from home, evident in the people-oriented Moon in Libra closely squaring Jupiter in their wedding chart. With Jupiter also in fruitful Cancer, Noor and the King had four children together between 1980 and 1986, and Queen Alia's three children also lived with them.

The Moon's sextile to Neptune and Jupiter's trine to Uranus rising in the wedding chart helped Queen Noor find and support her own causes in Jordan. One of her priorities was helping those in the west better understand the Arab world. She went on several speaking tours of the U.S. in the 1980s and accompanied the King on many state visits. Noor's goals included improving the lives of the women and children of Jordan. She also established official organizations supporting nature conservation, culture and historic architecture, and personally worked on their behalf.

Unfortunately, though, the frustrations of Mars conjunct Saturn became clear, and the Moon conjunct Pluto in the marriage horoscope brought complex situations to the family as well as the country, since the Moon also represents one's country and the public, and Hussein was its head.

As might have been expected, there were some conflicts between Noor and some of her many step-children. It took years for her to feel that the people of Jordan accepted her, and she was later criticized for over-spending and her lack of fluency in Arabic. There were even rumors that her marriage had not worked out. There continued to be tensions in Middle East politics, with Jordan placed literally and figuratively between Israel and the Arab world. While Jordan had tried to move toward a more democratic system, by the end of the '80s its economy was also not doing well.

King Hussein had also misjudged Iraq's Saddam Hussein, hoping he could persuade him to resolve his issues with Kuwait peacefully. After Saddam invaded Kuwait on August 2, 1990, international forces were sent in. Soon, refugees from the Gulf Crisis swarmed into Jordan, adding an extraordinary 25% to its population of 3.5 million. Then in 1992, King Hussein's doctors found a precancerous growth and he had surgery at the Mayo Clinic in Minnesota, being assured that the problem was resolved.

Back in Jordan, Hussein met with Prime Minister Yitzhak Rabin of Israel to address some of their conflicts, and they signed the Washington Declaration at President Clinton's invitation in July of 1994. Hussein was hailed for his role in this historic event.

King Hussein was diagnosed with non-Hodgkin's lymphoma in 1998 and returned to the U.S. for chemotherapy, with Noor by his side for several months of treatment. While there, he was invited to join President Clinton's Wye Summit, and participated in the negotiations between the new Israeli Prime Minister Benjamin Netanyahu and Yasser Arafat of the PLO. He was nominated for a Nobel Peace Prize in 1998 for his life-long efforts toward peace, but returned to Jordan to die on February 7, 1999.

Queen Noor lived in Washington D.C. while her children attended school, and subsequently spent time in the U.S., England and Jordan. Her autobiography *Leap of Faith* was released in 2003. She serves many charities, continues to lecture, and speaks out on issues of importance to the U.S. and the Muslim world, including terrorism. She never remarried.

While we can see many of the challenges Queen Noor and her husband faced in their wedding chart, her T-square involving Jupiter, Uranus and Neptune is at the heart of her continuing need to strive for international understanding and tolerance. King Hussein's horoscope, likewise, with its significant Venus in Libra rising, a cardinal, angular T-square, and two yods with Uranus in the eighth house, made for someone who would constantly work toward peace but who also needed to adjust to the many vicissitudes of the life he was born into.

Notes and Sources:

Brau, Jean-Louis, Weaver, Helen and Edmands, Allan, *Larousse Encyclopedia of Astrology*. New American Library, New York, 1977.

Christino, Karen, *The Best of Al H. Morrison*. Stella Mira Books, Brooklyn, New York, 2006.

Dellios, Hugh, "Widowed Queen Noor's Future Cast in New Light." *Chicago Tribune*, February 9, 1999.

Geyer, Georgie Ann, "American-Born Lisa Halaby Returns to Washington as Queen Noor of Jordan." *People.com* archives, June 23, 1980.

Naina, "The Four Wives of King Hussein." *Royalista.com*, August 25, 2014.

Noor, Queen, *Leap of Faith: Memoirs of an Unexpected Life*. Miramax, New York, 2003.

Raatma, Lucia, *Queen Noor: American-Born Queen of Jordan*. Compass Point Books, Minneapolis, 2005

Wikipedia.org profiles of Queen Noor and King Hussein

The Astrology of Royal American Marriages

While it's always fun to look at the horoscopes of the rich and famous, I began this project with the idea that I'd find significant Jupiter and Saturn influences in the birth charts of the Americans who married foreign royals. In Jupiter we find the experience of the exotic, new lands and different languages. Saturn brings status and responsibilities. But my analysis of the ten birth charts of these brides and grooms also turned up some surprises.

Jupiter is the most obvious planet to begin with, since its keywords of travel, expansion, luck, fame and wealth are evident in these life stories. Interestingly though, Jupiter plays less a part in these horoscopes than expected. The Duke of Marlborough had Jupiter sextile his Moon, as did Wallis Simpson. Hope Cooke had Jupiter sextile her Sun and King Hussein had Jupiter conjunct the Sun. (We cannot consider houses since several of these horoscopes have uncertain birth times.)

Jupiter in combination with Pluto is the most common aspect for the greater benefic, with seven out of the ten spouses having Jupiter-Pluto aspects (70% of the charts). Wallis had the sextile, the Duke of Windsor a wide conjunction, Hope the square (also a little wide at 7°), Prince Rainier and the Chogyal of Sikkim the trine, and both Queen Noor and King Hussein of Jordan shared the trine aspect in their birth charts as well. Four out of five of the wedding charts also share this planetary coupling: Consuelo's wedding had a sextile between Jupiter and Pluto, Wallis' an opposition, Grace Kelly's a conjunction and Lisa Halaby's a square. All of these combinations suggest that these people learned something profound from their contact with other cultures and that their experiences transformed their beliefs.

Jupiter is configured with Uranus in four of the ten natal horoscopes: the Duke of Marlborough had Jupiter conjoining Uranus, Grace Kelly had Jupiter sextile Uranus, and Prince Rainier and the Chogyal shared the trine. With this planetary combination, a uniqueness of outlook and openness to new experiences allowed them to take unusual paths.

Jupiter is the traditional ruler of Pisces, along with Sagittarius. And while Pisces and Sagittarius are by no means the most represented signs in this group (Sagittarius is actually one of the less common) the royal couples have notable examples of both signs. The Duke of Windsor, Grace Kelly and Hope Cooke all shared the Moon in Pisces. Consuelo had the Sun, Saturn and North Node in Pisces; King Hussein had Saturn in Pisces and Queen Noor has the North Node in this watery sign. (Prince Rainier and the Chogyal shared Uranus in Pisces, but they were born in the same year and this is more of a generational placement, lasting approximately seven years.) There is something all-embracing about Pisces and those with placements in this sign might not perceive the inherent boundaries of their situations as others may. (Aquarius, for instance, the least represented of the signs in these charts, might not tolerate a restrictive marriage.)

The other Jupiter ruled sign, Sagittarius, also showed up in several places. Prince Rainier and perhaps the Duke of Marlborough shared the Moon in Sagittarius, with the obvious connotation that they were internationally-minded as well as willing to gamble. Both visited the U.S. to claim their brides. King Hussein of Jordan, the only major player in the international scene of this group, had Jupiter in Sagittarius, giving him openness and a broad understanding. Grace Kelly had Saturn in Sagittarius; a simple keyword description of this placement might be an international career.

A proliferation of the sign of Libra surprised me the most. Of course, while we would hope and expect to see the sign of partnership turn up in the horoscopes of those with notable marriages, it's an astrological truism that we can't anticipate consistency; similar characteristics and life experiences are often indicated by various signs, houses and aspects. Despite this, however, *every bride and groom in this study had important placements in Libra.*

Consuelo and Wallis both had the Moon in Libra — putting a high value on partnerships like marriage. Hope Cooke had the Ascendant in this sign. The Duke of Marlborough had Venus in Libra. Grace Kelly had Venus in Libra conjoining her Scorpio Ascendant, and King Hussein had Venus conjunct his Ascendant with both in Libra. Venus in Libra is placed in one of its ruling signs. Love and partnerships may become an art form in a sense: these people really know how to have a relationship.

Even more surprising was that four of the ten partners had Saturn in the sign of Libra: the Duke of Windsor, Prince Rainier, the Chogyal and Queen Noor. Although the Prince and the Chogyal were born the same year, this seems like quite an unusual number of charts with this particular planet and sign combination. In traditional astrology, planets are strongest in the signs they rule or the signs of their exaltations, and Saturn is exalted in Libra. All of these individuals were known for both their positions in life as well as their relationships.

Saturn in Libra gives us people who take all relationships seriously; they're a responsibility not to be taken lightly. Saturn in Libra may also strengthen a person's position in life. Each of these four royals also had Saturn in "good" aspects: the Duke had Saturn trining Jupiter and Neptune; the Prince, Saturn trine his Sun and sextile Neptune; the Chogyal (another Gemini born only eight days before) had Saturn trine his Mercury and sextile Neptune; and Queen Noor has Saturn sextile her Mars.

Another notable placement in the group is Mars in Capricorn, the sign of its exaltation. It's intriguing that one of the most common essential dignities in these charts is associated with the serious, status-oriented planet Saturn. Consuelo, the Duke of Marlborough and King Hussein all had Mars in Capricorn, giving them the ability to restrain their impulses and consider before acting. (Consuelo's mother Alva Vanderbilt also had this placement.) Mars in Aries is of course its ruling sign, and Wallis and her husband shared this placement. Although they were both over forty when they married, their union nevertheless appears to have been the most rash or ill-advised: they seem to have allowed their passions to rule.

I often look for essential dignity and it can be found in abundance in these horoscopes. In addition to the Venus in Libra placements previously listed, the Duke of Windsor, Prince Rainier and the Chogyal all shared Venus in Taurus, its other ruling sign, and Queen Noor has the Moon exalted in Taurus. While the three Venus in Taurus men each had some issues with money, they ultimately attracted wealth. Wallis Simpson, Prince Rainier and the Chogyal all shared Mercury in its ruling sign of Gemini; Queen Noor has Mercury in Virgo and the Sun in Leo. King Hussein had the Moon in Cancer, and the Duke of Marlborough had Saturn in Capricorn.

Another sign most often represented is Scorpio. This complex and pragmatic sign, which relates to personal transformation, joint finances, inherited wealth and estates, seems a natural fit for these royals. The Duke of Marlborough and King Hussein both had the Sun and Mercury in Scorpio and Grace Kelly the Sun, Mercury and Mars. (The Duke may also have had the Moon in Scorpio.) Prince Rainier and the Chogyal had Jupiter in Scorpio and Wallis Simpson, Saturn.

Destiny seems to play a strong part in the lives of those born to royalty as well as those who marry into it. How much is indicated in the horoscope? How much is free will? While contemporary astrologers like to assert that we can control our fate, experience suggests a different perspective. In over twenty years of advising clients the best way to handle astrological influences, I most often found them following the path of least resistance in their horoscopes (and I, too, am the same as everyone else). The selection of wedding dates tends to be what the bride ends up with, despite an astrologer's intervention. This may be different in Hindu countries, but there the entire match might be dictated by an astrologer, with the bride, herself, having even less control.

Saturn is prominent in many of these horoscopes and those with a stronger Saturn may experience more restrictions in their lives. 40% of these royals had Saturn in Libra. Consuelo had Saturn conjunct her Sun, and her Duke had Saturn conjunct Mars in Capricorn. Wallis and King Hussein had Saturn squaring Jupiter; the Duke of Windsor, Saturn trine Jupiter; and Hope Cooke, Saturn conjunct Jupiter. These combinations could be seen as somehow karmic, but we don't need to believe in reincarnation to see that they may also impose limitations on freedom and choice.

The Lunar Nodes, so intrinsically related to eclipses, can also be used to analyze the role that destiny plays in life. Judith Hill in her book, *The Lunar Nodes*, says that, "In metaphysical tradition, the Moon has always symbolized the soul's journey in-and-out of incarnation. Therefore she carries the bundle of memories, preferences, and experiences that the soul has absorbed" and, "The nodal knots can thus be seen as two points where our souls are tied and knotted into the wheel of life, our Earthly incarnations" (pages 4-5).

How do the Nodes show up in the charts of these royals? Eight out of ten of them had a Node conjunct a planet or personal point in their birth horoscopes. Consuelo Vanderbilt, with probably the strongest Nodal connection, had Saturn exactly conjoining her North Node in Pisces, with the Sun also conjunct her North Node. She married on her exact nodal return, shortly before turning nineteen, and had little control over the men in her life until after her Saturn return. Her husband the Duke of Marlborough's Sun was closely inconjunct his North Node.

Wallis Simpson's Gemini Sun was about 2° from a trine to her North Node in Aquarius. The Duke of Windsor had Mars conjunct his North Node in Aries and both trined his Midheaven. At their marriage, the South

Node in Gemini conjoined her Mercury and Neptune and his fifth house Jupiter and Neptune. She may have been blind to the outcome of the union; he could only see its positive aspects.

Grace Kelly's South Node in Scorpio conjoined Mercury in her first house. The Prince's South Node in Pisces conjoined Uranus in his tenth house. At their marriage, the South Node in Gemini conjoined her Jupiter in her eighth house and conjoined his Sun.

Hope Cooke had the North Node in Libra closely conjunct her Ascendant. The Chogyal had the South Node conjunct his Uranus (like Prince Rainier). At their marriage, the North Node in Cancer conjoined her tenth house Mercury and Mars, and also conjoined his Sun.

Lisa Halaby was born with the South Node conjunct her Mercury and the North Node trine Uranus. King Hussein had a stationary North Node in Capricorn conjoining his Mars in the fourth house and trining Neptune. When they married, the North Node in Libra conjoined his Ascendant and Venus as well as her Saturn. This is another relationship in which destiny seems involved. Could Lisa have said "no" to the King's proposal? Given who she was and the trajectory of her life, I think the answer is No, just as Consuelo accepted her mother's decree as we would expect from her chart. Both of these women, by the way, also had the North Node in Pisces.

And what about the odd coincidence of Prince Rainier and the Chogyal being born within about a week of each other? I hadn't noticed this fact until I began the overall chart analysis, having first studied the various couples and their marriages separately. They had vastly different lives and situations, and their weddings were seven years apart. But each married wealthy American women, had three children by them, and gained great publicity as a result. What might the odds be, out of ten people, that two had such unusually similar life experiences? Without a birth time for the Chogyal we unfortunately can't go much further astrologically.

Of course we could say that the aspects and placements of the Nodes are what brought about such significant events in all of these royals' lives. But isn't that in some sense similar to fate? We see these people living out their lives within the pattern of their horoscopes. Or do things "just happen?" I leave it to the reader to decide.

Notes and Sources:

Hill, Judith, *The Lunar Nodes: Your Key to Excellent Chart Interpretation*. Stellium Press, Portland, Oregon, 2009.

About the Author

Karen Christino has written horoscope columns for *Glamour*, *Cosmopolitan* and *Life & Style* magazines, as well as features for *Marie Claire*, *Seventeen* and numerous astrology journals. She was the astrologer for *Modern Bride* for nearly ten years and wrote the "Choose Your Career" column for *American Astrology* throughout the '90s. Karen has a B.A. from Colgate University, also studied at Columbia University, and is professionally certified by the National Council for Geocosmic Research. Read her blog and more about her work at *KarenChristino.com*. Karen's books include:

Your Wedding Astrologer

Filled with wedding tips for each sign of the zodiac, *Your Wedding Astrologer* helps brides plan the perfect affair and understand a new spouse, in-laws and sexuality. There's even a chapter on choosing wedding dates astrologically.

What Evangeline Adams Knew:
A Book of Astrological Charts and Techniques

The astrological secrets of America's most famous astrologer: how Adams predicted World War II and the stock market crash of 1929, foresaw death for Enrico Caruso and Rudolph Valentino, and chose presidential winners, travel and wedding dates. Includes chapters on Evangeline's work with the magician Aleister Crowley and for clients like Edgar Cayce, Joseph Campbell, Eugene O'Neill and Tallulah Bankhead, along with court transcripts of her famous New York City fortunetelling trial.

Foreseeing the Future:
Evangeline Adams and Astrology in America

This one-of-a-kind biography tells the colorful story of a woman who defied convention as she single-handedly popularized astrology in the U. S. Adams wrote four best-sellers and had a top-rated national radio show in the early 1930s. She battled legal authorities in New York City for the right to practice astrology, married a man over twenty years her junior, founded a tremendous business enterprise, and made stunning predictions.

The Best of Al H. Morrison

The collected works of one of the most brilliant and innovative astrologers of the 20th century. Morrison's thoughts on Chiron and the minor planets, the Void of Course Moon, Declination, and a wide array of other topics in astrology and beyond.

More at *KarenChristino.com*